T0165166

ACCIDENTAL
INTERNATIONALIST

ACCIDENTAL
INTERNATIONALIST
Memoirs of a Businessman

Alan S. Colegrove, PE, PhD

ARCHWAY
PUBLISHING

Archway Publishing books may be ordered through booksellers or by contacting:

Archway Publishing
1663 Liberty Drive
Bloomington, IN 47403
www.archwaypublishing.com
1 (888) 242-5904

Interior Image Credit: Linda Colegrove

ISBN: 978-1-4808-7865-5 (sc)
ISBN: 978-1-4808-7866-2 (e)

Library of Congress Control Number: 2019906564

Print information available on the last page.

Archway Publishing rev. date: 8/16/2019

For my mother, the journalist, in memoriam.

For my aunt, the great globe-trotter.

For my children and grandchildren—hopefully an insight into what I was like when I was too young to be an Opa.

Contents

Acknowledgments

I want to thank my deceased parents for setting me up financially to allow me the time and experiences to write this book. My mother was a lifelong journalist, and I wish that she was still around to read it. I also need to thank all those individuals who I reference but do not name—shipmates, colleagues, customers, bosses, and subordinates—whose association with me helped create the vast majority of the stories contained in this book. I have tried to obscure many of the stories and still get the point across. Hopefully, some of you will read yourself into the stories with a chuckle. The stories are to the best of my recollection, and I would not swear that they are 100 percent accurate. I want to thank Archway Publishing for a chance to get a book out to the public and for their well-organized method for so doing. Finally, I want to especially thank my wife. She not only devoted countless hours to the artwork through its many iterations, but she also patiently read and reread the draft manuscripts to add new ideas for material and keep me from going too far afield. Since I was tired of endnotes and pages and pages of references needed for a truly academic treatise, all other historical or situational facts presented are publicly available via an easy search on the World Wide Web and are not otherwise attributable.

Introduction

I did not start out to be an international businessman. Rather, I initially started out to be a mortician. After that, a marine biologist specializing in squids. After that, a Naval Officer with a desire to command a submarine. All those things that a kid dreams while growing up—in my case, in Dallas, Texas. But my international trek did begin there. It is funny how you can look back on your life and go, "Wow—how the heck did I get here?" And that is what I have done. This book is about my inadvertent trek into becoming a die-hard internationalist. I will cover how I got into the business and how I stayed in the business, and I will pepper the book with stories of my experiences, both from my Navy days (which were relatively short) and from my thirty-plus years in the international defense and aerospace industry. I will include many lessons learned and cultural stories as well. Having lived abroad three times in my life for collectively almost fifteen years, as well as having more than another decade devoted to international business, I have a lot of both—lessons learned and cultural interactions.

International business is not for the faint of heart. You have to be willing to go outside your comfort zone in many respects. You need not give up your core values, unless your core values are very judgmental of the differences in other cultures. One example is holding hands with another male. I was raised a Texan, and my personal space is about three feet in all directions unless you are family or a known female. But in many cultures, it is perfectly acceptable as a sign of respect and trust to hold hands or offer cheek kisses with the same sex. I knew it was absolutely the highest honor when one of my northeast Asian colleagues grabbed my hand and walked me down a long boulevard. We were on our way to meet his wife at their home—an unprecedented honor as well since in this part, as in much of the world, business meetings were held in restaurants, not at homes. But my skin still crawled because in Texas you just don't do that—that is, hold hands male on male. In the Middle East, with representatives and customers you had known for years, you absolutely had to do the cheek-kiss thing—three or four pecks. I could never figure out how many exactly. But once you were in, you had no out—peck, peck, peck. Germany, handshakes all around; Middle East, cheek pecks; East Asia, hand-holding. You learn to adjust, or you fail in international business.

The following is an introduction to an American life lived internationally. I attempted to group the stories chronologically, but sometimes that is hard to keep within specific subjects. Unlike domestic business, which of course has plenty of government interference, international business has even more government interference—very significant interferences, especially in high-technology areas. You must learn to cope with the Washington, DC, process as well as overcome internal company shibboleths on the topic of international business and international assignments. Most companies just want the money, not the hassle. A colleague based overseas had spent a week escorting a very senior vice president to meetings, and while in the limousine on the way back to the five-star hotel on the final day of the visit, the vice president sighed and said, "Why can't they just give us the money and pick up the equipment on the shipping dock in the US?" What the heck did he expect? This is exactly the attitude that torpedoes US business efforts abroad. Your leadership needs to be willing and able to engage other cultures. Otherwise, just stay domestic and save the costs of an international staff.

I remember the story a different business-development colleague told of finally getting a division president to a country besides the UK; he went, grudgingly, to Italy. And he had a great time! The food was great, it didn't make him sick, and the people were polite and delighted he took time out of his busy schedule to fly all the way to Rome for several days of meetings. Surprise! Much of the world outside the US is just as nice as in the US—and, in a sense, even more appreciative that you take the time to visit and do business. If none of these appeal to your leadership, just accept the reduced earnings and stay domestic. International business, while rewarding in the end, can make you look old before your time. It is the dogged pursuit of foreign contracts and relationships that have helped make our country the best source of hope in the recent world economic order. Hopefully, we will not let future generations down as some of them also pursue such an occupation.

Chapter 1 will cover my early international and general cultural experiences I had around the world. Chapter 2 will move into my first major international business assignment as well as raise issues associated with export and travel security. Export is an extremely important and complex issue, and while I will summarize and give my experiences, it is best left to experts, either in your company or from outside consultants hired to train you. Chapter 3 will cover my first long-term civilian expatriate business assignment as well as discuss more aspects of culture, especially those that move further away from our American experience and cover being an expatriate. Chapter 4 will cover my years of international-on-the-go globe-trotting around well over a dozen countries but based in the US. It is also the period I started my doctorate in the rather obscure aspect of international trade called offsets and countertrade. Chapter 5 will return to my second extended expatriate tour in yet another interesting and rather more dynamic geographical area. Its sidebar topic will be corruption experiences and ways to avoid it, as well as discussing the experience of setting up an overseas branch office. The leading US law on corruption, the Foreign Corrupt Practices Act (FCPA), is a powerful tool in the hands of the US Government, and I also advise getting a good course on it if you plan on much international business. Chapter 6 will return me to the US in the unusual role of being the American working for a small foreign firm as well as seeing me finally set up my own business with a focus on offsets and countertrade— business that is exclusively tied to international exchanges—and some lessons learned on that.

I hope you enjoy the journey. I have.

Sailing into the unknown world of international business.

CHAPTER 1

Early Life
Early Experiences, First Looks at Culture, and Navy Days

The only international trips I had done before the age of fifteen were the occasional ducks across the Texas-Mexico border, led by my parents, to do a little shopping. There's not much to report on that. But on entering tenth grade, I started my first official foreign language: German. It was at the conclusion of my first year's study that I got selected for a chance of a lifetime: a six-week summer exchange in Germany. I have a knack for picking up languages, and although my vocabulary after a year was smallish, my enunciation was excellent. My German teacher selected me for a program run by Volkswagen that took high school kids from around the US and matched them one-on-one with employees' kids and arranged for most of the costs of getting both sets exchanged. There was not a bunch of us, of course, but enough to fill a major tour bus. My German counterpart arrived first for about a week's overlap. Then off I went to Wendschott, Germany (near Hanover), for six weeks, with my counterpart catching up with me for a final week there. To paraphrase a great American president, John F. Kennedy, from his famous West Berlin speech, "Ich bin ein Wendshotter!"

In the mid-1970s, this was the start of my cultural indoctrination. I made my first major mistake: not arriving dressed like a Texan! My host family, watching all the kids get off the chartered bus, was looking for a guy in a ten-gallon hat wearing chaps and sporting a six-shooter. I merely came off in jeans and a rugby shirt. Now that I have double the number of years outside Texas as in it, I don't feel the pressure anymore to say "y'all" and "howdy." But I still regret not having had the foresight to at least look Texan on the first day.

From that arrival, we went right into dinner and discussion—with a dictionary at my elbow much of the time. I later learned the mother actually spoke English well. She seemed to always know the English equivalent for food items on a restaurant menu, for instance. But they were under orders to make me speak German, and for six weeks, that is what I did.

The first evening delved right into the heart of the issue: they wanted to know where I stood on Communism. Though I have softened a bit over the years, I have always been slightly to the right of Attila the Hun when it comes to politics. We quickly established that I was okay in their book. It turns out the father had fought as a teenager in World War II and been taken prisoner on the Eastern Front in the collapse of Army Group Center. That was in the spring of 1944, and he is lucky to have lived. To start with, only about 30 percent of the soldiers survived to become prisoners of war. Then it was more than five years after the war ended before he was released, all that time performing manual labor to rebuild the Soviet Union. He said the first indication his family had survived the war was a single postcard with nothing on it but a return address. His ancestral home was now deep in the new Poland, under Communism. After he was finally released, he returned there and married at some point. But they wanted to get to the West. They ended up near Berlin after a few years and started a routine of crossing into West Berlin to visit friends. About two months before the infamous Berlin Wall was raised (i.e., in the summer of 1961), they left East Berlin for the final time. They had just two suitcases—one with clothes for a weekend and the other full of toys for my counterpart (about age four at the time)—left, and never looked back as far as I can tell.

Border Walls

There I was … I'll use that phrase a lot in the book, as that is the way most fighter pilots start a story, and for my active duty time of seven years, I was a fighter pilot.

Anyway, the town of Wendschott is very close to the (now former) border between West Germany and East Germany. In an amazing microcosm of the Cold War, I got to watch it grow.

During my first visit in 1973, the border was barely barbed wire. I did see East German guards with dogs on the far side of the fences—and I do mean far, as that no-man's-land had to be a hundred yards or wider. My next trip came during the summer of 1979 on my German exchange at the Naval Academy and subsequent month of vacation. This time, the border had unscalable fences well over twenty feet high and guard towers every so often. My adopted family had driven me to take a look at the changes the intervening six years had wrought. I did not pace off the tower-to-tower distance. As we turned around, our lights flashed across a man-made canal/moat; the closest tower turned off its interior lighting, which had been visible moments prior, and turned on a strong searchlight—right on our car. This, of course, scared the heck out of the family and even registered in me as a higher-than-normal risk. Off we went. I was later told that the turnaround probably looked like an attempt to pick up someone attempting an escape from East Germany.

Moral: The Cold War is over, and the wall is down, but many regimes still take a dim view of border security and associated crossings. Be careful out there.

So they had valid reasons for wanting to know where I stood.

The only other event that night was learning to drink German wine and playing absentmindedly with their new little kitten, who really enjoyed me. But when we stood up to head for bed, the mother shrieked. My arm that had been playing with the cat over the edge of a comfortable armchair was shredded by the sharp little claws and teeth. I was cleaned up and disinfected—no harm, no foul—but I made sure to separate cat play and wine a bit more.

The rest of the stay was delightful. The temperature was a bit cool for summer—cold by Texan standards—but otherwise great. I was taken to see as many sights as they could cram in between the father having to work and driving distance, as well as several military visits with family friends in the current German military. We got to Hanover, Helgoland Island (where I had a nasty head cold that was somewhat mollified by a buttered rum drink), the North Sea (jeez, cold), and a couple of military bases, which was a nod to my interest in anything military. I got several uniform pins for my representative German World War II *bauer's* (farmer's) hat—a hat worn during the final years of the war, as more costly hats and helmets were unavailable. It was based on the long-standing farmer's hat with pull-down sides to protect the ears. I wore that hat all through my remaining high school days, and it became an intense object of theft by my well-intentioned female friends. I did continue to jog every day and got to help in their garden, harvesting potatoes and strawberries.

Only two things really stood out to my new family: the fact I showered every day (they did so two or three times a week) and that I ate my ice cream cone in seconds. They thought that was way too fast for my health.

On my counterpart's return, though, he quickly explained my peculiarities in these regards. He said Texas is so hot in the summer that you sweat just sitting and that everyone takes a shower every day—sometimes twice if working outdoors. And that same heat means you have to eat your outdoor ice cream in a flash—or end up wearing it as a sloppy mess.

Because my overlap with him came at the end of his time in the US, I also got to hear his impressions of the US in general and Texas in particular. The one that most vividly stands out is how big he found everything. He had taken an 8 mm movie camera along and had the film developed on his return. In one stretch, shown before friends and family, he had shot about ten minutes of east Texas interstate highway through the front windshield. There was absolutely nothing in the clip except tall trees, an occasional highway sign, and the road. As he ran it, he said, "This is just a short clip. We would drive for an hour or more and see nothing else."

This brought many exclamations of disbelief from the crowd. How on earth could so much empty land exist? But he assured them it did and this emptiness was common, at least in Texas. By now, I could put this in perspective. You could not drive ten minutes in Germany without coming across a small village.

We remain friends, if at a distance. Years later, our two families worked out their own informal student exchange. My brother went over for several weeks at one point, and his sister came to our place for several weeks not too many years after that. I was in Pensacola, Florida, at that point, starting my pilot training. My parents brought her down, and we took her to the Gulf of Mexico. Her first comment on entering the water was "This is like a bathtub!" Yes, the Gulf in a Floridian summer, compared to the North Sea in a German summer, would seem like a dip into a warm bathtub.

Body Language

There I was, an American in Denmark with the German Navy on a midshipman first-class summer-training cruise. Now the Danes still do not fondly remember their occupation by Germany in World War II. On our first day in port, we had to wear uniforms. I was exploring downtown, drifting into and out of shops. It was readily apparent that the locals were not too keen to see me walk in the door … until I spoke. I quickly learned to just stick with my English. As soon as they realized I was American, not German, they were all smiles, handshakes, and taste this or look at that.

One evening, several of us went to the local discotheque. We were now in civilian attire, but we were clearly marked as foreigners. After chatting a bit amongst ourselves, I started looking around the place. At one table there were five lovely young ladies … all staring straight at me. Taking the hint (which is remarkable—my wife says I am exceptionally dense when it comes to these things from women), I wandered up to the one on my left and asked if she would care to dance. She gave me a huge grin but said no and looked to her friend on her left. I asked that lady, got the same grin and no, and looked at her next friend. On I went down the line until the final gal was reached. When I asked *her* to dance, she hopped up with a big grin and in beautifully correct British English said, "Absolutely." Turns out she was a British lady visiting her Danish friends for several days. They had quickly marked me as an American and were trying to figure out how to get my attention to come over, dance, and chat with their friend. We had a delightful evening dancing and chatting before I finally had to head back to the ship for an early-morning departure. And her husband was a Formula One racecar driver …

Moral: It is sometimes good to be the foreigner; don't be the obnoxious American, but be the polite American!

With the exception of a high school graduation gift of a week in London with a class trip, I stopped really thinking about international until well into my time at the Naval Academy. I figured the Navy would certainly give me a chance to see foreign ports. Midshipman cruises helped a bit. My first cruise (between freshman and sophomore, or per Navy lingo, plebe and youngster, years) got me to Vancouver and Juneau. Well, Juneau is not a foreign port, obviously, but it was certainly in the middle of nowhere. Getting there, I got stuck on a watch station on the fantail (back) of the ship for almost four hours. Turns out my scheduled relief was sick or otherwise unavailable, and I was asked to keep watching in case someone fell overboard. No one did. But it was a scenic cruise up the various mountain- and tree-lined channels to Juneau. While there, I went with some locals to watch the fireworks on Independence Day—from above! We hiked up a mountain to do so. Before we left, I saw one of my hosts stick in his coat something that approximated a Dirty Harry Magnum .44 pistol. I asked what that was for. He said, "Bears." I asked if that would kill one. "No, but it will sure piss it off, and it will chase me while you guys run fast in the other direction."

My only other Alaskan story is getting to invade an island. It was about three in the morning and bright as it could be, being June. The midshipmen were handed unloaded rifles and put in World War II–style landing craft and went ashore as a diversion. But when the gate of the landing craft dropped, we were still a good twenty or thirty feet from the beach! A few of us were saying, "Whoa—a little farther, please," when a nasty-sounding Marine sergeant barked, "Out of the boat *now*!" In we went—waist deep in freezing water. But ashore we went—lasted about an hour, then were reembarked. I ruled out Marines and stuck with my number one reason for going to the Naval Academy—to be a submariner.

I had placed out of two years' worth of German courses, courtesy of my excellent high school German teacher and my exchange trip's practice. I took the final two courses as humanity electives and started attending the German club from time to time. Our final summer's training at the Academy was to go to sea for four to six weeks as a junior officer. A limited number of midshipmen could volunteer to do this as an exchange student, which I did. And that is how I got back to Germany again for a month, this time in the German Navy. Five of us went to Germany and were divided among four small ships. I was fortunate to be the only American on my vessel, so it was easy to stay in German the entire time. It was another fascinating experience. I followed around my guide, stood watches, worked on torpedo firing solutions (and got them correct, somewhat to the surprise of the ship's captain), and dropped depth charges, during which I was almost swept overboard, as the seas that day were incredibly rough and the depth charge releases occurred off the low aft end of the ship. The other officer and I had to cling to the aft gun to keep from being knocked off our feet as three feet of angry green North Sea washed over the fantail. We also hit ports in Denmark and the UK. At the latter, I was asked to give a ship's tour to visiting firemen, the Germans figuring I had the native English thing down pat. I did, from bow to stern, discussing the weapons and paying special attention to the firefighting and damage-repair equipment on board. The captain and a couple of the officers followed along politely without saying a word. After the tour and a round of refreshments (that is, some German beer and sausages), the firemen left. At this point, the captain turned to me and said, in German, of course, "Wow—you did a great job—and you actually had it all correct!"

Learning the Language

There I was … fast-forward a decade and a half, and I was working on another foreign language—and a tough one: Finnish. I was calling the Finnish Air Force Headquarters like I always did early one day each week to talk with my counterparts.

Finnish is one of those isolated language groups without a lot of native speakers. It is apparently related to Hungarian, though when I was in Hungary later, it didn't sound all that related to me. It is spoken as it is printed (unlike French or English), which makes it easy to read aloud a word—but its uses of endings to change tenses and make conjunctions makes it difficult to learn. It always follows its rules, as one Finn told me, but the problem is that there are so many rules. Now, all Finns have to learn both Finnish and Swedish, the two national languages, and the vast majority go on to learn a third—often English. I gave it a try to learn Finnish, just being polite.

Turns out I did okay—conversationally. I was on a street corner at one point, and a Finn must have asked for directions. I replied politely in Finnish that I couldn't speak Finnish. He laughed and asked again. I switched to English and got an amazing open-mouth stare … and he wandered off to a real Finn. Back to the air force. At one point about a year in, they started asking me to step out of the meeting when they switched to Finnish for a private conversation. The other Americans asked if they should all leave, and the reply was, "No, only Alan, as he is beginning to understand too much Finnish." Forward another year, and they stopped asking me to leave. I asked why, and the reply now was, "We trust you completely."

Anyway, I would call the headquarters once or twice a week with something to ask or relay. I would ask the receptionist (back when the world had real people answering phones), in Finnish, for one of my contacts. He would pick up, we would chat, and then he would say, "Hang on a minute. So-and-so wants to chat." After him might come a third person, or even a fourth. One day, out of curiosity, I asked how everyone knew I was on the line. The reply, "Well, the receptionist places you on hold. We have a small office, so she just yells across the office, 'The American who speaks Finnish is on line one for Jukka.' Then we all know it is you and head to his office." I commented I didn't speak Finnish all that well, and they said, "Yes, maybe so, but you are the only American we have ever met who is even close."

Moral: Even making an attempt at the local language generates huge benefits in international relationships. You may not have the gift of languages, but making an effort is always appreciated.

As part of both Germany trips, I was exposed to a lot of Germanic culture and history. My foster parents, for instance, drove me to Berlin. Now, we are knee deep in a Cold War, and my Germanic parents were refugees of it and West German citizens by ... luck? I should have asked. Especially because one of my German "brother's" high school friends had escaped from what was then Czechoslovakia and was not allowed, for instance, to go on a high school class field trip over the Berlin wall because he might be arrested and imprisoned. We were going early to Berlin—to beat the traffic. I distinctly remember the border. Four passports—German (okay), German (Alles in Ordnung), German (okay), US—whoa! The guards gave me a very guarded look (sorry—couldn't help the pun) and charged my foster family an extra twenty or thirty Deutsch Marks for allowing me the privilege to ride to Berlin on the only open road—by treaty—through East Germany (technically, the DDR—Deutsche Demokratische Republik). Of course, once in Berlin, we did an East and West city tour. But because my family was German and I was American, for the Eastern City tour, I had to go through Checkpoint Charlie, and they went somewhere else. All I remember from that trip is that a cute Spanish gal talked with me a fair bit of the trip, and the goose-stepping honor guard of the Soviet soldiers in front of their memorial for the fallen.

How Not to Say "Good Morning" in Finnish

There I was ... watching my delightful but woefully non-linguistic boss introduce us during a tour of Finnish Air Force Bases to announce the upcoming arrival of the F-18s.

Now, don't get me wrong. The Finns were very pleased to have my boss as the program head. However, after a couple of years of working on it, he still could not order even a beer in Finnish when in-country. Having a great sense of humor, when we did the informational round, he decided he would start each presentation with a greeting in Finnish. He failed miserably. However, he also got the point. So, after the first attempt, he would start with "'Hyvaa Houmento,' which is an American attempting to wish you 'good morning' in Finnish." (Pause) Then the room would erupt in laughter, as the Finns did get the joke—he was so poor at Finnish that they did not know what he was saying until he translated it into English!

My next boss on this program was even more problematic. His last name was Finnish origin—yet he also could not, after two years in-country, order anything in Finnish. We were at a party at his house not long after he returned and took over the program. I asked his delightful wife if he could sing at all. "Not a chance. He can't carry a tune in a bucket!" Hence my current belief—if you cannot sing, you cannot learn to properly enunciate a foreign language, and for languages where that enunciation is critical to understanding, you will fail.

Moral: In international business, be willing to laugh at yourself and put yourself a bit out front in local culture. Most places will think it great!

Back to my final summer training at the Academy. I was with the German Navy. I was dropping the depth charges off the back of the German ship and going to both Denmark and Britain. I did win the bottle of Sekt (German champagne) for guessing closest the time of the trip through the Kiel Canal. With that and the departure gifts, I had more wine and schnapps than I could carry legally on a plane ride back to the US. But I still had about three weeks … on leave (vacation) … to meet my brother and my foster-German brother for a road trip through Central Europe. What pair of parents in their right mind lets three mid/late-teenagers off on a road trip in Europe? Obviously, my parents and my foster parents. I do remember on the train ride to join my family and brother that a nice, older German lady basically chastised me for the withdrawal of US troops in 1945. Why did we not stay? (Umm, obvious agreements that in hindsight were probably less than helpful. The Yalta Conference had effectively divided up postwar Europe into either liberated countries or spheres of influence—Western and Soviet. With no stomach to fight yet another world war, the Soviets were allowed to occupy what was to become Eastern Germany and rule as they desired.) It was one of the most insightful and disturbing conversations I had on a German train. Why did we not stay? The lady said that the Americans arrived first. They very carefully searched the houses—gently lifting the blankets to look under them and the bed. And they almost always left behind chocolate bars. When they withdrew, per treaty, the Russians were not nearly as gentle. She did not elaborate, but I have read the after-action history—not very gentle. Hence, a nice, older lady chastising me for something my grandparents had been somewhat a party to.

Off we went on a poor boy's tour of southern Germany, Switzerland, Austria, Liechtenstein (*Tritt Nicht Danaeben, Tritt Voll Hinein*). We were mainly hitting youth hostels. I remember several well. The first was a converted fortress on the Rhine. We had to haul mattresses from a dank room. The next I can recall was a beautiful place overlooking an Italian lake. The final two were a mixed pair in Munich—one about World War Two era and the other like a new Holiday Inn. To the former of those, we had to catch the late subway back—with bursting bladders. We had gone to a tourist *hofbrauhaus* for beers—and each of us bought one round—a liter a piece. Jeez. What with singing various touristic national anthems (Japanese stuck out), we had missed a chance to be more … comfortable … on the trip home. My German brother was already back on beer by midday, while my brother and I stuck with Shandys.

My German brother had been a border guard during his mandatory service. We were returning to Germany from Switzerland or Austria, via a back road in an attempt to avoid the traffic. We had to get into a line of cars, and this was making him fume. What was the holdup? Now, travel in Europe midsummer is notoriously bad. But my German brother had little patience. As we pulled up to the checkpoint (well in advance of the European Union, by the way), we saw a Volkswagen van pulled over and all the luggage outside being inspected. Two hippie-looking late-teens or early-twenties were standing by the opened luggage. But when we three terrorist-aged males pulled up to the checkpoint, my German brother lit into them like they were the cause of global warming. He got out of the car and yelled at them for about five minutes—and we were just waved through. Yes—don't pay attention to that twenty kilos of weapons-grade plutonium in the trunk (that's a joke). About ten minutes down the road, when my friend had cooled a bit, I noted what he had forced—and he paused, thought, and laughed. Yes, we had just gotten through a border with zero inspection on what should have been a suspect car, saving us probably an hour's delay.

Back to accidentally becoming an internationalist. I had ruled out the Marines after wading waist deep through ice-cold water to invade a US island. I stuck with my then dream to be a submarine officer. That required entry into the nuclear power program. To enter that program back then, you had to have an interview with Admiral Hyman Rickover. Rickover had promised Congress in the mid-1950s to personally interview every officer selected for the nuclear power service, and Congress held him to that promise—renewing on a special-case basis his commission and active duty status for one of the longest in United States Naval History. These interviews have since gone into almost a mythical status with antics such as "Make me angry" so a model ship gets smashed;

"Play something" as a horn is handed over the shoulder of an astonished midshipman; "Get in the closet" for maybe an hour or more. But he knew his business and created the safest nuclear power program in the world—and that on submarines that had to dive and live deep beneath the surface of the ocean, sometimes for months on end. I majored in marine engineering at the Academy—ship propulsion systems, really, with a heavy emphasis on nuclear power. I was surviving but not an academic star. Nonetheless, I thought my chances of getting into nuclear power were very good. That didn't work out very well.

Rickover Interview

There I was … my twenty seconds of infamy with the famous Admiral Rickover.

For the Naval Academy graduating class of 1980, there was a nuclear power draft. All midshipmen with a GPA over 2.0 went first to a pep talk in the evening a few days prior to the interview process. The pep talk was on Halloween. While we honored the day as usual with an evening meal in costume, all my buddies went back into uniform for the evening meeting. I deferred. "What are they going to do, make me go nuke?" was my quip. I was the only person in my company of twenty-six seniors who was going to volunteer for that program. With sword in hand and dressed in chain mail and cloak, I went off with my uniformed buddies for the talk. Great talk, by the way. Unlike many that night, our speaker was a great business-development guy: he emphasized the extra pay, the highest educated crews in the world, and the chance for real-world missions. Unlike most of the rest of the speakers who droned on about "needs of the Navy; like it or lump it!"

The joke was on me. During the real interview process, you started with a couple of very technical/academic interviewers. "Draw the equation for a cylindrical reactor on the board, please." Umm, not my strength. I wanted to go into submarines to sneak into Soviet ports, shadow Soviet ships, and duel with Soviet attack submarines. Each of these interviews took sixty to ninety minutes. Apparently, you usually got two thumbs-ups or two thumbs-downs out of these interviews. If there was a deadlock, you got a third interview. I got the third interview. Must have been a thumbs-down. Then I got the Rickover interview.

It lasted twenty seconds. "Why are you doing so

poorly the past three semesters?" There were a host of reasons, but my answer was, "Well, sir, part stupidity and part laziness." The admiral snapped, "Well, your first two years and your SATs show you are not stupid, and there is no room for laziness in my program. That is all." Pause. *"That is all."* Out I went.

A month later, we got the results: two of my company buddies (one of which, if I recall correctly, was a GPA 2.1 history major) were forced to go into the nuclear power program, while I, a GPA 2.8 marine engineering (i.e., nuclear power) major, was rejected. We went over the wall that night and got wasted. The next morning, I skipped classes and went to have my eyes rechecked; first time around on my commissioning physical, I had been twenty–twenty-five in one eye and not pilot material. This time, a very compassionate doctor whose husband was a pilot said, "You are on the borderline. I don't have the heart to disqualify you, but you will most likely fail down in Pensacola. But I'll give you twenty-twenty now." And that is how I became a pilot.

Moral: You never know when something bad happening to you is good for you until after the fact. Admiral Rickover did me one of the best favors of my life in rejecting me for the nuclear power program.

I dragged a dismal but passing senior year first semester up almost a point for the second and final semester—including in nuclear power classes, one of them taking the final exam sitting on the floor with my dying calculator plugged into a wall socket to complete the test. I finished that three-hour exam a full hour and a half before anyone else in the room … and improved my grade from a C (2.0) to a B (3.0). I learned that by meeting a buddy on the red beach—suntanning area hidden from the public by our huge dormitory complex of Bancroft Hall. I was in my swim gear on a towel, sipping a Mountain Dew, when I saw one of my classmates going back to his room still in class uniform. Apparently, everyone else had stayed to the bitter end (more nautical lingo—a "bitter end" is the end of a rope or line on a ship). He asked why I left so early, and I said simply, "I was done!" Yes, done with wanting submarines. Next chapter would be Navy Pilot.

Eye Checks

There I was … yet another pre–Navy Wings (i.e., flight qualification) medical. I had hoped to complete as few of these as possible before the end of my flight training, given my marginal vision. But ...

The Pensacola check referenced by the kind doctor at the Academy finally came. I think I didn't read a thing for three months and ate lots of carrots. I think I passed, but I will never really know for sure. The gent in front of me got into some kind of argument with the medical technician doing the eye check—he probably didn't make pilot grade in the eyes. Anyway, we were in a production line and needed to move on. The tech told me to sit and read lines nineteen and twenty (or whatever). I did as best I could. When I looked up, he was still looking down the hallway at the previous guy with a snarl on his lips. "Okay, fine." Scribble, scribble. "Next." Twenty-twenty.

A year later, I had to endure the test again. This time I was in a quiet, uncrowded office in south Texas. The tech had me read the lines. "Reread line twenty again, please." I did. "Doesn't that fourth letter look more like a C?" "Of course it does," was my quick reply. Still twenty-twenty. A year after that, a final annual physical just a month before I got my wings. "Read line twenty." I did. "Read it one more time." A laugh. "Oh well, you are too far along to flunk out. But you'll have glasses soon!" And he was correct. On having night carrier landing issues in the F-4 Phantom about eight months later, one of the conclusions was that I should get glasses, which I did. I did dutifully wear them in flight, though I would sweat so much there would be drops on the bottom of the lenses. But I also just gradually got better on instruments and with what vision I had. I still don't wear glasses.

Moral: Sometimes unexpected folks help you reach your dreams. Be polite and inclusive, not divisive. In the end, I never was good at night carrier landings, but at least I could remain safe.

How the heck did I ever get into the military? I grew up watching Walter Cronkite recite the body counts in Vietnam. The Tet Offensive was just another battle to be read about, and all the protesters on college campuses were before my college time. However, my dad had been a veteran in the Korean War—Navy Reserve Officer Training Corps (ROTC) into an LST (landing ship tank) that went over to help land equipment and move prisoners of war around. That experience—crossing the Pacific Ocean in a flat-bottomed LST—prevented him from agreeing to my mother's ardent desire for a cruise on a legitimate cruise ship for years. Of course, anyone who has been on a Royal Caribbean or Carnival Cruise line knows full well that "haze gray and underway" is entirely different from "all the food you want, and then some, plus live entertainment every night" (though my dad did get to watch a collision at sea caused by blackout conditions—but that is another story). It took about thirty years to get over those Pacific trips.

My grandfather had entered the Navy in World War Two as a chief of electricians. He had worked prior as a member of Florida Power and Light, and he joined in the patriotic call-up for the war. He served on a light aircraft carrier—CVE—abbreviated by the crew as Combustible, Vulnerable, and Expendable—the San Jacinto—named for the winning battle in Texas's war of independence (i.e., where I grew up). He got to watch torpedoes go under his ship headed for the big carriers; I think they had painted the side of the ship, "Big Carriers That Way," with a huge arrow (not sure the Japanese pilots could read English or cared at that point). My other grandfather, who I did not know because he predeceased my birth by several years, had volunteered for World War One (yes, the first one) as a Chaplain. He felt obligated to go with his boys from Ohio at an age over forty and served just behind the lines, helping the wounded by writing letters home on a portable, collapsible typewriter. My kids and I accompanied my mother to donate her father's typewriter to the Military Chaplin's Museum in Fort Jackson, South Carolina, when my kids were in college in South Carolina. So, going into the military, while not popular in 1976, was in the blood of my ancestors and, therefore, me. And both my kids, as of this writing, are serving officers in the US Military—Navy pilot and USMC adjutant—fourth generation.

While submarines did make foreign port calls, they were fewer and more controlled than surface ships, even big ones like aircraft carriers. Still, I did not figure on actually getting stationed in a foreign country. That is exactly what happened. I did reasonably well in flight school and was assigned to the last of the F-4 Phantom squadrons. These happened to be permanently based in Japan. All in all, that was about three years in Japan, cruising the Far East. I told folks I asked for "Fighters, East Coast, and forgot to specify the continent." The F-4 Phantom, by the way, was an outstanding aircraft to pilot into the international defense business. No one upgrades faster than the US, so Phantoms and their competitor equivalents were ubiquitous during much of the early parts of my international experiences. Several countries I worked with had air forces with Phantoms in them. Even after they were being replaced, many of the senior officers and engineers had all grown up flying and working on the venerable Phantom, and an instant rapport could be established with both senior officers and rank and file.

Why was there a US aircraft carrier and air wing based permanently on Japanese soil? Well, that goes back to the end of World War Two and the nonaggression stance the US (and much of the world) wanted to see out of Japan. Of course, the Communist threat was also foremost in many politicians' and diplomats' minds, and a recovering Japan would be vulnerable. The US therefore agreed to manage Japan's protection. Marine, army, air force, and naval bases were constructed or rebuilt. This was good timing for when first the Korean and then the Vietnam Wars came along and the US needed safe forward staging bases. After Vietnam, the US wanted to stage an aircraft carrier in Japan. The Japanese were hesitant. But as long as it was not nuclear powered (the Japanese have some bad experience with the blunt end of nuclear power), it would be allowed.

On the completion of Phantom training, my wife and I packed our belongings and went off to the Navy bases in the Tokyo metroplex. The first issue was base housing; there wasn't any available, at least for about a nine-month wait. But we were helped to find a delightful, if very small, detached house. And I do mean small. The Navy moved all our furniture from a standard two-bedroom American apartment, and it nearly didn't fit this two-bedroom, two-story house. The movers had to actually hoist some of the second-floor items through an upper window. It was relatively Western in layout, with wooden floors, not tatami mats, and Western toilets, not squatters. But it did have its quirks. First, no central anything—air-conditioning was two window units I had to install, and heat was provided by three or four kerosene-powered heaters. That is legacy of the earthquake potential; if they fall over, they are designed to shut off and hide the heat source from the fuel tank. We had our first earthquake while at the officers' club for dinner very early on. My wife hissed, "Stop shaking the table." I hissed back, "I'm not; that is an earthquake!" Boy did her eyes get big. She almost ducked underneath the table. Fortunately, fortune smiled, and we were spared anything more serious than a few very mild tremors during our time there.

For shopping, between the local stores and the base exchange, we were all set. I did get to see the most expensive grapefruit I had ever seen in downtown Tokyo. If I recall correctly, it was a single grapefruit in a lovely box for well over fifteen dollars. This was before camera phones, so I couldn't snap a photo. My wife had the story where she and a friend went into a clothing store and saw a lovely leather coat. Their first attempt at currency conversion flushed it out at a steal of a deal for fifty dollars. But then they redid the calculation adding the missing zero—$500! They slunk out of that store quickly.

Anyway, back to getting to Japan. My wife went straight to Japan. I went straight to the ship in the Philippines. I arrived in Manila with no clue of my next move, but fortunately I was able to join a friendly van full of returning sailors going to Cubi Point, where I thought I would find the ship. Wrong again—kind of. The ship had pulled out that morning. But as I am blearily checking into the officers' quarters for the night (this at about midnight), a warrant officer saunters up and asks if I might be Lieutenant Colegrove. Who the heck knows my name at midnight in the Cubi Point Bachelors' Officers' Quarter? Turns out he was a leave-behind for some maintenance activity, but he knew a "new guy" was to arrive very soon, and he knew the ropes and got me off to the carrier in the morning. My commanding officer had a huge grin when he saw me and my seabags appear in Ready Room 2 that morning.

Actually, when I say we spent three years in Japan, it was really my wife who spent three years in Japan. I was gone for about three-quarters of it, either on a training deployment (Korea, Philippines, northern Japan) or on the aircraft carrier USS *Midway*, off the coasts of those same countries or in the Indian Ocean. It was certainly an unexpected way to start our marriage. But in international living, you learn to expect the unexpected.

Expect the Unexpected

There I was … payback time for three days on the beach when I had a hydraulics failure off the Philippines and had to divert to (land at) a shore base. Yes, sitting Alert Alpha in a hot cockpit in the middle of a South China Sea day on the deck of the USS *Midway* (CV-41.) Alert Alpha is the five-minute response launch, and it means you sit in the middle of the hot day, or the middle of the cold night, in the cockpit ready to launch. As one of my departing comrades said, as we kidded him on missing us, "When I think I miss you guys, I'll grab a metal chair, a book, a flashlight, and go sit in my front yard at midnight for fifteen minutes in the middle of winter … and not miss you anymore!"

The joke was on the schedules officer, as we got launched! A free flight! Thank God for the Soviet Union, who decided that day to practice attacking a US carrier with some Badgers (a Tupolev Tu-16, officially). That is, by the way, why a bipolar world split was so convenient. We practiced against them, and they practiced against us. Think of all the taxpayer dollars and rubles saved!

Anyway, back to the story. Off we went. Four Phantoms stuck out in front of the carrier as it transited to Thailand. Just a routine day in the US Navy Foreign Legion. Now, Soviet aircraft have to be escorted when within a certain range of US assets (bases, carriers, etc.). That means a fighter or sufficiently aggressive aircraft on their wing at all times. They peeled back one of the Phantoms to fly that wing … but not me. I am hundreds of miles out in front of the carrier, and my closest wingman is back escorting the Badgers—which means I am totally alone, as the other two Phantoms are hundreds of miles to the south. How boring is that? It was so boring we decided to try to wash the aircraft by flying through some local cumulonimbus clouds in the hope that there were some liquid drops inside. Because of my station, I was also the closest aircraft to Vietnam's territorial waters. We had to keep scrupulous observance on that boundary to avoid an international incident.

Which is exactly what occurred.

We were being "close controlled" (yes, the quotes are there for a reason) by a surface ship—cruiser as I recall. They were reporting … nothing. Maybe some MiGs over Phnom Penh. Now, as a Navy Fighter Pilot, MiGs would be very interesting. But since they were airborne over a place hundreds of miles away, less so. So, chase a cloud. Or two. Or more.

Then …

"Switchbox 202, we have a contact off your starboard (right) side about five miles." Okay. Great. Give me a vector. No help. My RIO (Radar Intercept Officer, a.k.a. back-seater) was working the radar vigorously. The RIO then said, "Look a bit low and to your left." Bingo! Two aircraft. They looked like some errant Navy A-7s on a surface search patrol, but as we closed, they were two MiG-23 Soviet fighters! My RIO and I were rendezvousing on two Floggers!

Hot damn! We said, "Roger, contact two Floggers." The voice on the radio, previously a somewhat young and hesitant-sounding voice, changed immediately. "Confirm two Floggers?" growled an older, firmer voice. For the next few minutes, I had the absolutely best close control I had ever had in my life! Oops—they just jettisoned their drop tanks! That may mean they meant business. We started Hi and Lo Yo-Yos (a yo-yo is a maneuver that keeps your fighter at its optimum speed by going high and low behind an adversary while remaining in a firing position) while chasing them around. Best eight minutes of my short military career. They eventually stopped maneuvering and started flying back toward Vietnam. At the international border line, we did a reverse Immelmann (an upside-down 180-degree direction change by doing the back part of a loop) and exited with a low-altitude, high-speed flyby over the cruiser to clear our tail. We later learned they had been launched to check out one of our surveillance aircraft, and on maneuvering against me for several minutes had run almost out of gas. On landing (a "fair" 3 wire), I was given a gratuitous upgrade to an "okay" due to the excitement of contacting the enemy. The best part was that some months prior, a single Navy F-14 Tomcat had a similar engagement during transit with a single Flogger—and had not maneuvered to a position of advantage before it, too, ran low on fuel. This Phantom had gotten to the Commanding Heights on two Floggers.

Moral: Always expect the unexpected. When you approach a country, be prepared to adjust to the circumstances. Do what is necessary to conclude the deal given what you have in hand, without starting World War Three.

Our interactions with the local cultures varied. My wife, who can't speak a foreign language to save her soul, got through it with a pad of paper, a pen, and a smile. She has one story where she was in a local shop trying to find a particular item—medicine, soap, something. She approached the nice young salesgirl, asked if she spoke English, and got a definitive no. She then turned to look through the items with the salesgirl at her side. After reading a couple of products and putting them back, the salesgirl—without taking her eyes of the shelf—said in tolerably good English, "I think this is what you want." Just too shy to try it face-to-face. We traveled a bit in the country, including staying at a local hotel run by a nice couple whose son had studied in the US, so their English was fairly good (I never got past a couple of words of Japanese, having so little time in-country). While there, they humored my wife with her breakfast staples (eggs, bacon, toast), but they were more adventurous with me, having me try traditional Japanese and at one point stuffing a seaweed rolled rice ball down my throat (my wife said she'd have choked it up if they had done that to her).

And flying over one of the largest cities in the world in a high-performance tactical jet aircraft was interesting. Very often, after we took off, the Japanese controller would quickly ask if we were within visual flight rules—because he wanted to dump us off his frequency as fast as possible. Not being an airliner, we always asked for odd things that were hard for the controllers to understand. The sooner we were released, the happier Air Traffic Control was. Of course, it did impart to us a license to kill—well, at least make a lot of noise. We would fly over Mount Fuji and other ridges at low altitudes, circle an active volcano just off the coast, and generally buzz around burning gas and getting ready to return to the base. As for the family's international exposure, we added Hong Kong, Philippines, South Korea, Singapore, and Thailand to our visit list and capped it with a trip to Perth, Australia, where a cute, young Australian lady tried to pick me up right under my wife's nose on a wine river valley cruise; that didn't go very far, but my wife still remembers the attempt.

Being a Bad Boy

There I was … nearing the end of a shore deployment in Cubi Point, Philippines.

It had been a great almost two weeks of nonstop dogfights and bombing missions and low-level training in the lovely, warm Philippine weather, often in conjunction with our adversaries but brothers in arms in the US Air Force based up the road at Clark Air Force Base (this all pre–Mount Pinatubo eruption, which put paid to most of the US installations in that area). Toward the end of the week, internal squadron politics got the better of me and led me to a bonehead decision.

Almost every day, a leave-behind F-14 Tomcat crew from a squadron in the Indian Ocean would do a single proficiency flight. It was typically a low transition (that is, a flat runway run close to the ground) to an Immelmann departure (that is, lots of speed, pull straight up, and eventually be inverted going the opposite direction before rolling upright). Now, my maintenance crews, who seemed to think I was okay for a junior officer, had been egging me all the detachment to "show us something." So, on this particular man-up, as I was heading to my plane, I told the flight line petty officer after our routine exchange on this topic, "Watch this."

During the premission brief, after the usual mission-related items, I had said, "Departure will be a ten-second separation followed by a low transition to a pop-up aileron roll." (An aileron roll is a roll about the long axis of an aircraft.) No one apparently heard me except my wingman pilot, a grizzled Vietnam-era vet of very, very few words. We took the runway, and I thundered ahead, retracting the landing gear with just enough air under the plane to stay up, got absolutely as much speed as I could by the end of the runway, then popped up, did my aileron roll, and continued on. At about the ninety degree of roll, my back-seater asked,

"Do you have this (i.e., under control)?" I said I did. After we were upright, he asked, "Was this briefed?" I said as far as he was concerned, no. Apparently my wingman made one of his few ever verbal statements as he watched from behind on the runway. "My God, he's going to do it!" "Do what?" asked his back-seater.

I returned early with an aircraft malfunction, and no one was around to park me except the maintenance officer. As we were being chocked, he looked up, pointed at me with a huge grin, and in a silent query asked if I had done the roll. I nodded yes, and he gave a huge, grinning headshake with the mouthed "Oooooo." When I climbed down, he said, "Skipper wants to see you *now*." The skipper asked if what he had heard was true, and I said yes. "There is a C-130 (cargo plane) leaving for Atsugi (our home base in Japan) in forty-five minutes. Be on it." I made the flight. It was a cargo-only flight, and I was the only passenger, so after takeoff, I got up and went and slept on a pallet the whole way. My wife was delighted to have me home three days early, and her only comment was something to the tune of, "So, you are finally acting like a fighter pilot!"

I later learned a couple of things. First, all the maintenance troops were watching with great expectation and cheered as I did the roll. Second, the commander of the air wing happened to be manning his aircraft just as I took off and also saw the aileron roll. He, however, did not cheer. In fact, according to his navigator on that mission, he did not say a word for over three hours—not on the flight, not during the mission debrief with the air force. It was only when the communication line with the air force debrief was shut down that he stood up, turned to the assembled strike package, and said, "I cannot believe the gross violation of safety and regulations I just witnessed."

To end the story, I was grounded for a month. I stood a lot of watches, much to the sniggering relief of my buddies. In the end, I went to Captain's Mast—the Navy's underway nonjudicial punishment system. It was then that I realized my past performance had been widely recognized throughout the air wing. Air wing staff and other squadron senior officers were stopping me with a smile and telling me not to worry. The officer in charge of the investigation stopped me in one of the passageways a couple of days before the Mast with a smile, saying I was probably going to get a letter that looked very much like one he was intimately familiar with. The Mast was conducted in whites—a uniform we didn't wear very often underway. It was a short and direct one-way conversation. But the gist was that, with a severe but not official warning letter (currently hanging framed in my office), I was to return to flight status. It probably cost me my 300 Midway Trap and 1000 Phantom Hour patches (ended with 279 traps and 972 hours), but it really did boost my reputation as a fighter pilot among both fliers and maintainers—and that is not all bad!

The PS on this is that several times over the later years, I ran across the commander (eventually an admiral before he retired). His bottom line: I was too good to go unpunished, as he couldn't let me be a bad example for the rest.

My next skipper only asked me one thing as he took over the squadron: "Any more aileron rolls inside?" "No, sir!" "Then get back to work!"

Moral: Several on many levels. Do a good job, and it is noticed. Be aware of internal organization politics and play them as needed. In international business, you are likely to be an outlier and need to find those internal champions to keep your name fresh and your next assignment and promotion opportunities reflective of your performance.

Everywhere I went those early years, I tried to be part tourist. I wanted to see what was important to the locals. I kept the same philosophy through my many years of international business. My favorites were, of course, often the country's military museums. Archaeology has also always held a fascination for me. One memory is of the Grand Buddha in Kamakura, Japan (not far from where we lived). One day, we were there as my artist wife took pictures of the statue for what would eventually become a lovely framed photo on the house wall. But as she turned around (I had been assigned to stay out of the way and hold the backpack-sized camera bag she used back then), she could barely see me—surrounded by a dozen or so Japanese high schoolers all practicing their English. She got a shot of the moment with all of us bent down over our dictionaries, working out an answer to a complicated question they had asked me in English. Most places have something to see. As part of international business, you need to have this curiosity. It can actually be important to your business. I know after my first year or so in Malaysia, I had seen more of their country than most of them had. Same with visitors to the US. My on-site Finland counterparts in St. Louis were always asking me about places in the US to which I had never been. They were going to see them before they left.

See the Country

There I was … meeting again with embassy staff, as I was well known, and they wanted what I knew. This time, they passed along a great local story. Their commercial staff had recently had to unmess a problem created by a US business visit.

A businessman flew in for a meeting on Friday that got unavoidably delayed until Monday. On Monday, he went to meet the prospective client. The client (a CEO) started by apologizing profusely for the delay and schedule disruption, which the American graciously responded to as not a problem. Then the local asked how the businessman had spent the weekend.

The reply was, "In the hotel room, doing email."

The CEO stiffened and said in summary, "You traveled thousands of miles to my country, had to spend a free weekend here, and saw nothing of a country in which you have never been to before? This meeting is over." And he walked out.

Moral: Everyone is proud of their country; not investigating it as a visitor is an insult. I have always made a point of visiting something; in my line of work, generally the military museum, but anything will do. Even an afternoon's city tour bus, or a visit to the local history or art museum, or shopping at a souk/bazaar is a story to tell, not only at home but to your newfound local counterparts.

We left Asia after seeing everything we could within a day's drive of Tokyo, plus several other places by train and a half dozen cities in other countries. We had to semismuggle our cat out of Japan. Not out of the country, where we complied with all the regulations on shipment of animals, but into and out of our final night in Japan. By the way, that is a topic to be addressed: your beloved pets and shipping them around the world. We did it once, but we did not do it again, preferring to find loving homes for them to stay in the country we were in. There are companies that specialize in the transshipment handling, but it is a somewhat risky proposition for the animal. Do your research on that. Also, company relocation policies may not cover the cost, which, while not a king's ransom, is also not cheap.

We were in the Navy Lodge for our final night in Japan. It had a strict no-pets policy. But we had nowhere to keep a cat, at least for our very early departure from the base in the morning to Narita—three hours away by van. We snuck her in and spent a sleepless night hoping there would be no loud meowing. Got it done! My wife, who was seven months pregnant at the time, got up after takeoff and laid down in the middle of the coach section's seating across four seats. Buckled in, she didn't move for the fifteen-hour flight (this back when most airlines didn't overbook, and the flight was practically rented by the US military anyway). I also left it on a minor note in Naval Aviation history.

Smoke and Mirrors

There I was … ready for my absolutely last flight in the venerable F-4 Phantom II. Off the USS *Midway*. But, little did I know it, a flight into (minor) history.

The *Midway* was headed for a major upgrade due to the transition to the F/A-18 Hornet, and the Phantoms were being retired from active service in the US Navy. While this was not the last Navy flight of a Phantom, this launch—off the shores of Korea—was the last active-duty Navy carrier launch of the Phantom.

A first gaggle (gaggle is a bunch of unsupervised Navy pilots leaving a carrier and desperate to get home) had already launched an hour prior, along with a slice of all the other aircraft in the air wing. As this was somewhat historical, there was a small crew from the military press (*Stars and Stripes*) on board document-ing the final moments of the Phantom. They had been particularly interested in our sister squadron, taking several interviews and filming them a bit.

This had not gone unnoticed by our maintenance Master Chief. Unbeknownst to me, he had personally decided to make sure one of his crews made that last catapult launch. The day prior, a good buddy of mine, Ichabod (he looked for all the world like Ichabod Crane of the *Headless Horseman* Disney movie), had asked the Master Chief how he might be in the last Phantom launched from the *Midway*. The curt reply was, "Be in Mr. Colegrove's back seat." So, sure enough, Ichabod (then the schedules officer) made sure that he and I were paired for the return to the shore. Just so you know, he did not mention this until after we were airborne.

We manned up on a clear spring morning off the southern coast of Korea and got ready to go. However, after starting, we had a problem. Our pneumatics appeared to be broken. In the Phantom, you used the pneumatics for, among a few other things, the critically required extension of the nose strut for proper launching—no nose strut extension, no launch. I was looking at zero on the cockpit pressure gauge. Now, the sister squadron, who desperately wanted to be the last Phantom launched, had an apparent hydraulic problem. The Navy safety wonks had years prior figured out that you should have hydraulic fluid colored red so a leak would be immediately visible. So as plane after plane launched, I sat with no pneumatics, and the now-competition sat with a stream of red fluid coming from a nondescript fitting.

Enter the Handler. Handlers handle all the aircraft on an aircraft carrier. They typically are only slightly less annoyed than the Air Boss, who handles all the planes flying near an aircraft carrier. Therefore, you do not want to piss them off. After all the other aircraft (A-7s, A-6s, E-2s, other F-4s) had gone, the Handler had only two aircraft left … yes, me and the sister squadron Phantom. The Handler sent over his Master Chief to check the stories. Sure enough, I had no pneumatics. But with a quick swipe of a towel, the other Phantom's "leak" was "fixed." And off it went. As soon as that other aircraft hit full burner on the catapult, my pneumatics made a miraculous recovery! Turns out the maintenance Master Chief had had one of the folks carefully loosen one fitting, and by tightening it back up, I was good to go in about five minutes.

Moral: International business (and offsets, a subset thereof and my specialty) can be a bit like attempting to make history: appearances can be deceiving, you have to trust others to do their part well, and when successful, you get the credit. Just remember all those who helped.

The Navy certainly did a reasonable job moving folks around, but of course the Department of Defense has made that a two-hundred-year-plus skill set. But even then, all the junior officers in the air wing had to gather together to bend the ear of a visiting admiral to complain about getting an overly large number of crappy orders. That is what helped get me to Key West as an adversary pilot rather than south Texas as a primary flight instructor. My final year was as a semi–*Top Gun* instructor, fighting the latest in Naval Aviation with an aircraft designed in the 1950s … and often winning! It is amazing what an old tool can do in the hands of an experienced wolf. I can recall a couple of stories. Once, when I was in a single-seat A-4E Skyhawk in a rolling scissors (up/down tactic trying to gain a firing position) on an F/A-18, the other pilot, an F/A-18 instructor, was cussing me out for being so difficult. In a guns-only ploy, he was not able to get to the firing solution with his twin General Electric engines and computer-automated, high-rate-of-fire gun! The other was in the relatively benign TA-4J adversary/trainer Skyhawk, during which flight I had a hundred-degree fever. I was the least-sick pilot on a detachment critical for training and was ordered to help complete the training objectives of the day's missions. We had a left-to-left pass, but I, not wanting to pull a lot of Gs, had dropped my airspeed low and pulled through a semiloop for a firing solution. I heard the instructor, incorrectly keying the external verses internal microphone, "Do you see him? Back there! Back there! Oh, Christ!" Next radio transmission, "Mullet, do you have Talley? (Talley means "sight of the enemy")?" "Yes, continue … Approaching Guns solution." Pause. "Pipper's on, Pipper's on, guns kill." When we got back to the debrief room, I was asked politely by the instructor for my view of the flight. I drew it on the whiteboard and then went and laid down in an empty room for an hour to recover before my next flight. The poor student emerged about that time with a really hung-dog look. I felt sorry for him. To be beaten by some of the oldest aircraft at the time—but that is how you learn. Our time in Key West was only a year, a very enjoyable year, with the birth of our first child. When I checked in, my new commander didn't care about my status but about the boat I could bring to the floating party, which the squadron threw two to three weeks a month either for us or to entertain flight crews who were in town for training by our squadron. I remember the second soon-to-be squadron commander's comment: "Oops." Stretched too far between docking and pier, he fell full faced into the warm, if dark, Key West water. But then he reasoned he needed to drink himself dry! But it was soon to end. Partway through the tour in Japan, my wife had said, "Pick me or the Navy." I decided for my wife.

Anyway, as that airliner was rolling down the runway in Japan, heading home to the US for good, we said, "Well, it has certainly been interesting, but we'll never be back in this part of the world again."

Wrong.

Export regulations are so complex they may seem like a crapshoot.

CHAPTER 2

Falling into International Business
First International Business Exposure,
Personal Security, Exports

After concluding my final year in the Navy in Key West, I parted from the service. It did take most of that final year to find a job, which I did as an engineer with a major defense contractor in St. Louis, Missouri. Off we went, with some regret, from my final posting in Key West to St. Louis, and settled into a typical, mid-American domestic life. That lasted all of about nine years, during which time I did squeeze in a master's in engineering management at what I liked to call "gradual school," as taking it one class a semester at night, it was truly gradual. When I finished that, I said I'd never take another course again that I didn't really have an interest in. The first (and only) follow-on course while in St. Louis was Scientific Methods for Dating in Archaeology. Now, about this time, having been doing a decent job around the place, I was called one day into a senior program director's office and asked if I would consider applying for the position of integration engineer for the recently won Finland F-18 Program. When someone that senior asks you to consider applying, it really means *apply now*. I did and got the position. I knew absolutely nothing about international business, nor what being an integration engineer for an international program entailed. I also knew very little about Finland, outside of the Winter War and Continuation War they had fought with the Soviet Union in/around World War Two. This was, timing wise, right after the breakup of the Soviet Union, so things were changing radically in the larger world.

International trade has, of course, come a long way since its early origins. But why would any sensible person, community, or country go too far out on a limb to actually go abroad in search of trade? The original long-distance international route was, of course, the Silk Road—a patchwork of routes between China and the Middle East. For millennia, goods have moved—with frequent interruptions by invaders—perilously along the route in both directions. As ship design improved, an alternate route out of the reach of raiders from the steppes in Central Asia came to form in the Indian Ocean, bringing especially the spices of Indonesia and India into the Arabian Peninsula by boat, crossing the narrow land of the Roman, Persian, Sasanian, or Muslim empires, and thence into the Mediterranean Sea and Europe. Pax Mongol opened the Silk Road periodically for the caravans into the Black Sea and the early Russian kingdoms as well as the Middle East via Persia. But in the late 1400s, the Ottoman Empire closed off all rivals with a choke hold on the routes through the Near East, all the way from Istanbul through the Holy Land and into Egypt. Whether by caravan via the Silk Road and its tributaries, or by boat via the Persian Gulf and the Red Sea, goods still had to transect the Ottoman lands, towns, and ports. The Ottomans then did what all good monopolies do—greatly increased the tariffs and taxes for transshipments in both directions, including spices to Europe. This drove the costs of the luxuries of the Orient through the roof. That made finding an alternate route to them suddenly of fiscal interest to many European kingdoms—hence the Age of Exploration. (Frankly, from what I have read, most of the discovered peoples and kingdoms new to European eyes either didn't want to be discovered or rued their discovery within a generation or two.) Western Europe began to explore and trade, because it helped the national balance sheet, and it made some merchants rich. And that is why we still go international. Your domestic market is saturated, or the competition is so intense that you can no longer make the high margins you once could with your product or technology.

Think out of the Box

There I was … with my trusty RIO (radar intercept officer) in an F-4 Phantom on a beautiful, clear flying day in
the Indian Ocean (that was a piece of luck; most of these
stories start with "It was a dark and stormy night …").
International business is often about thinking out of
the box to solve the situation in which you find yourself,
either on purpose or accidentally (the latter especially if
you have inherited someone else's pursuit).

So here is an out-of-the-box Navy sea story …

We taxied to the catapult for launch, gave the
thumbs-up, then were hurled down the bow at a speed
approaching 200 mph (320 kph). But partway down the
catapult stroke, the aircraft started shaking violently.
Once airborne, we were not climbing. Instead, we were
barely keeping our launch altitude of sixty feet off the
surface of the ocean as we struggled with whatever
issue had been thrown at us. We calmed down as our
eyes focused, and I saw the left engine at what is called
sub-idle, meaning not generating any thrust. As we de-
bated what to do, the right engine's fire light began to
glow, low at first but eventually brightening up. Now, in
a two-engine aircraft, to have problems on both engines
is a bad thing.

We contemplated briefly jettisoning our ordnance,
but that would have created a safety report and a black
mark against the squadron. Even though it would have
rid us of thousands of pounds of weight, my RIO and
I decided to gut it out, as we were at least not sinking
lower. We eventually got rid of enough fuel by dumping to climb high enough with the engine on fire and
get speed enough to shut down the stalled engine and
restart it—which fortunately restarted just fine. We
now pulled the burning engine back to idle, and the fire
light dimmed, then went out. Which was even better.
However, the plane needed to go back to the carrier
ASAP. So, we called the Air Boss (senior officer who
owns all the airspace within a few miles of an aircraft
carrier, much like an airport control tower) and requested the quick return, and he said in his usual gruff
fashion, "Make it quick."

Now comes the out-of-box part. The Phantom carried about eighteen thousand pounds (8000 kg) of fuel on
launching, but it could only land with about six thousand

pounds (2700 kg). So even after the bit of flying and fuel dumping we had been doing, we had ourselves a ten-thousand-plus-pound problem. At maximum dump rate, that would take fifteen to twenty minutes—not, we assumed, the Air Boss's definition of quick. Enter the one good GE (General Electric, God bless you) J79 engine we had with an afterburner burn rate of ten times the dump rate. After getting more altitude for safety, we hung the aircraft up in a slow speed / high angle of attack maneuver and proceeded to single-engine afterburn all that fuel in about five minutes. Came back and landed no problem (and maintenance found and fixed all the issues—we had not been hallucinating). No "thanks for being quick" from the taciturn Air Boss but also no getting called upstairs to get a dressing down from the Boss.

Enter another crew that won't be mentioned by name. They also had some issue right after launch and wanted to come back—engines were fine—maybe generator or hydraulic failure. The boss again said, "Make it quick." They spent upward of the twenty minutes dumping … and dumping … and dumping and got a fine dressing down by the air boss on their return for taking so long that they messed up the day's launch and recovery schedule.

International business can be a bit like that trouble off a catapult launch. You get thrown into it and wonder, *How the heck did I get here, and what am I going to do about it without having the boss chewing my reputation into nothing?*

Moral: In international business in general (and offsets, my specialty in particular,) you have to learn to think out of the box—change your approach, try a new and different idea. Your boss may not sing your praises, but at least they won't chew your rear off.

Of course, there also needs to be some technological advancements and some reasons for the other to want to trade. For Europe, sources differ, but uniformly, the figuring out of the magnetic compass for ship navigation was one of the major breakthroughs. Others varied, such as gunpowder (military advantage over potential trading partners), improvements to ship navigation via astrolabes and other latitude and longitude measuring devices, the improved art of cartography, improvements in finance structures (such as joint stock ventures that spread the risks across multiple companies), and even paper—for keeping accurate accounting records as well as recording navigation and the cultures and products encountered so that follow-on adventurers and traders knew what to expect. Note that several of these advancements were actually Chinese in origin—leading to the great question of why it was not China that sailed west rather than Europe that sailed east. But I will stick with becoming an international businessman. There was gold (and silver) in those lands, and for those who survived (many did not), they became rich and occasionally famous.

"Going international" evolved through the ages. The 1500s were mainly exploratory except for getting all that gold and silver out of the Americas. The 1600s saw the introduction of outposts around the world, where Europeans traded with locals and competed with their other continental brothers for access and territory. By the 1700s, trade was a foregone conclusion in almost all the world. Even the closed countries of China and Japan had a few licensed ports for those products from overseas. All this trade made Europe rich and powerful, and in the 1800s, this wealth and power was used to divide up the unorganized world and force open the last of the closed societies. International trade was at a historic peak prior to World War One—which didn't stop Europe from descending into that morass. The Great Depression hammered global trade and led in many ways to World War Two. After that, we finally got to the postwar era dominated for much of the past seventy years by the US, and in the past thirty or forty by the rise of Japan, the European Union, China, and the newly industrializing and emerging countries. With annual global trade currently in excess of US$20 trillion, it is small wonder that companies dream of entry or enlargement by going international, and they act on those dreams by sending employees—temporarily or permanently—overseas. They need adventurous people now as they did back in the 1500s. We just have the luxury over our predecessors of better vaccinations, quicker and safer trips, and the internet and Skype.

My first foray into international business was supporting my company with a major fighter aircraft sale to Finland. Finland had been very careful to pursue a neutral course since the end of World War Two. One aspect of this was buying top-line military products from a mixture of neutral and Soviet suppliers. Events such as the Helsinki Accords of 1975 and even the end of the first Gulf War were held in Helsinki, Finland, as a neutral place for the superpowers. However, as the Soviet Union crumbled and the Berlin Wall fell, Finland finally felt a chance to expand its supplier base. This was manifested in its largest military procurement to date: replacement of its frontline fighter aircraft. Previously split between (neutral) Swedish DRAKEN and Soviet MiG-21s, it sought to have a standard fleet throughout its air force. The competition was fierce, with the now-Russian Federation offering up either the MiG-29 or Su-27, the Swedes offering the GRIPEN, and two US firms, the well-proven F-16 and the F/A-18. In the end, the Finns selected the F/A-18 (for them—no A, as they did not want to attack anyone). It was the first Western fighter since World War Two (then mostly German aircraft) and the first US Navy aircraft since the Brewster Buffalo prior to and during the Winter War. This led to my opportunity to be the integration engineer for the various technical changes for that program.

My first trip to Finland was in November. I was joining a large number of program folks working on logistics planning. I think I was just sent to get my feet wet, so to speak (frozen, more correctly), and start building rapport with the Finns. As I was joining the group midsurvey, I flew alone into the town of Rovaniemi in far northern Finland. At least this was better organized than my arrival in Manila a decade earlier. I knew the rides, the hotel, and so on all in advance. I really liked working with the Finns. They were quiet and decisive. Once they had taken measure of you, if they liked you, you were included in their group.

This is probably as good a time as any to address security issues closely associated with international travel. You can count the times in the future stories that I did not properly follow my own advice and the advice of the experts both in and out of government. First, whether living permanently or traveling temporarily overseas, you can and should get on the Department of State's "advisory for citizens overseas" email list. It is usually pessimistic, but it does give an overall view of threats to US citizens, whether criminal, health, or terror. Also, State has the STEP program (Smart Traveler Enrollment Program). In it, you enter dates, flights, hotels, and the basics of where you are going and why. This helps State count citizens in a country when the emergency occurs. That is one reason hotels overseas want a scan of your passport—so they know which embassies to call in the event of an emergency. Entering the data can be a bit of a detail hassle if you have a long and complicated itinerary, but it is well worth the peace of mind that it provides. For those living overseas, you register with the local embassy or consulate so they know where you are for the same reasons.

Airport security has changed radically over the years. On my earliest trips, you could kiss goodbye at the airplane door and be welcomed at it. If you have not seen one of the early scenes in the movie *Up in the Air*, as a frequent business traveler, you must. Clooney is going through security with his novice supporter played by Anna Kendrick. With absolutely no disrespect, Clooney describes why he wants to be behind Asians in a security check: "They pack light and have a thing for slip-on shoes." "That is prejudiced!" says Anna's character. Clooney replies, "No, it is stereotyping—faster—my mother used to do it!" I have gone through (or not through) security accidentally with scuba diving knives, bottles as gifts and water, and small pocketknives—all based on the level of screening a country is doing. You will find some countries' airports tighter in security than others. That is why a direct flight to the US nowadays will have a second screening—just in case.

On landing, your first hurdle will generally be the immigration line. Sometimes they are fast, but sometimes, even in the US, they are slow. I remember a one-hour wait in Riyadh, though I was lucky. My boss recalled watching two entire movies on his iPad once. This is another form of security, as countries try to prevent undesirables from getting in and harming their own citizens, let alone foreigners. (Riyadh had greatly improved the final couple years. They even had immigration agents with a sense of humor—very unusual.)

Getting into and out of Israel

There I was … leaving Israel yet again. No disrespect intended for Israeli customs or security—just a story.

My first trip had been as a family vacation. Now, an American family with two preteen kids does not look like much of a threat. We were in line at security to fly from Egypt to Tel Aviv at something like ten o'clock at night. The security was very strict. What we saw as we were going slowly forward was a twenty-something male having his luggage checked carefully but politely (as far as we could tell) by security. We were in line maybe half an hour, got forward, got a very desultory luggage check, and were off to the lounge. That kid was *still* having his luggage searched—including the rolled-up socks.

My follow-on trips were all business. Israel has good technology, and in my companies at the time, Israeli firms had internal supporters who wanted me to check out the potential for offset use as well as reverse flow of technology and collaborative investments. So, I made several trips and visited a number of companies spanning much of the country. On one of these trips, I made a rookie mistake.

Not sure if this is still done, but to *leave* Israel back then, you had to have a letter from your local partner or visited sponsor indicating you had been on legitimate business. I had forgotten this until the eleventh hour. My sponsor said they'd get something to me that afternoon, which they did. But idiot that I was, I did not print it out; it was, after all, on my iPad in nice, clear print.

I did not make the rookie mistake of trying to clear all the customs and security at the airport on my own. You can buy a guide or facilitation service to get you through the process at high speed, and I highly, highly recommend it. (This service is, in fact, offered in many countries. Check it out, at least on the first trip.) Anyway, my guide was a little four-foot-something lady, who met me at the airport door and dragged my butt to the front of every line—and there were some three or four lines to be mastered, if I recall correctly. She would elbow folks aside, stomping on toes if needed. She had to have a night gig in the Israeli special forces, as she wasn't taking grief from anyone. We got to the point where you had to show the letter from the sponsor. I whipped out my iPad and handed it over. Chaos arrived. "No printed letter?" Well, no—they had emailed it, and here it is. They (the security and my escort) wandered off with the iPad and returned in a couple of minutes. The iPad was not good enough. At this point, I really didn't have any options. On a total whim, I opened my briefcase and pulled out a baseball hat given me by the partner company. I don't even recall why it was there. They probably just gave it to me as I was leaving, and I crammed it into the briefcase. But this time, hat and iPad in hand, off went security and my escort. They returned with an "Okay to go."

Moral: Keep those baseball hats in your briefcase until you get home—and don't forget to print out letters. For a laugh, check out a YouTube video under the key words "Israeli Passport Control Funny."

There are plenty of sources for what you should do to prevent making yourself a target for common thieves or angry terrorists. The first— which I frequently violated myself—was to vary your routine. You are not supposed to drive out of your abode and always make the same right turn toward the office. My big fault was always staying at the same hotel when I traveled, both in Southeast Asia and in the Middle East. I found a place that was convenient for the representative, had a decent gym and a decent restaurant, and stuck to it. Fortunately, most locations I went to were relatively safe. This, of course, is a huge no-no in international travel in risky areas. In my Southeast Asian assignment and most (but not all) of my Middle East jobs, I had no risk to really be associated with. But if you are headed to some areas with more … interesting … security situations, you need to adopt the habit of randomness. Your local friends may have no reason to dispatch you, but if you stand out, others might. The few times I went to the higher-risk areas later in my career, I was either accompanied or guarded.

Going to Yemen

There I was … I had a retired Marine Corps officer on my staff, and I had asked him to go to one of the most dangerous countries in the region at the urgent invitation of our local representative. As brave a Marine as he was, he was justifiably nervous. To make him feel better, I said I'd go along. What was I thinking? This was, by the way, about three months before the start of their devastating civil war. We landed in Sana'a and were immediately met by the representative's folks—two black SUVs, each with two folks a piece packing heat. We got to the only hotel that was considered acceptable for Westerners—nice, set back, extensive security. For the next three days, we had an amazing series of meetings with senior government officers and a great tour of the town. Not a single traffic light. With two cars driving at as high a speed as the roads allowed, even our rep after one ride (in the other car) said he was carsick and couldn't imagine how his guys did it.

We were treated to a very respectable representative office. The ministries we visited were, on the outside, a semidisaster, but as soon as you were inside the gates—peace and beauty. The final dinner with the representative was in downtown old Sana'a in a gloriously restored four-story townhouse. Stunning. We watched a wedding next door from the fourth-floor roof of the townhouse. It is such a shame that everything is probably gone in the civil war. Sana'a's architecture was very unique. Also, the cuisine was the spiciest my colleague and I had experienced in the Middle East. As Texans, we could really relate. I am hoping for a full recovery for that impoverished nation.

Moral: Sometimes risk is rewarded. Sometimes situations arise that prevent the reward. Just be careful about what is under some of those rocks you are turning over to find the gold.

Such is a partial issue in international business. In Malaysia, it helped to have outstanding local drivers who were exceptionally patient and organized. I remember one of the few times my Penang driver was organizing a lot of transportation for me and had to send a colleague to fetch me from the airport. The colleague's nicer car broke down, and he met me at the airport in a panic. How was he to get me appropriately to my nice hotel? He did have a non-air-conditioned pickup truck, so in we climbed, my luggage in the back, and went off with the windows down through the tropical afternoon heat to the hotel, arriving in time to shower for the early-evening meeting.

More Excitement Than Needed: Into a Really Big Sandbox

There I was … asked by an important and responsible representative to get myself down in person to see the difficult conditions they were facing installing our equipment on the international border. Flight to a location, four-hour drive to the hotel. It was a hotel, but the AC barely worked (this was August in the Middle East), and the shower—I don't even know if it had hot water, but at that temperature, it did not matter. Internet—go dream.

It was all a picturesque drive, first up the mountainous slopes through the fog zone to the plateau, then on through the desert to the final location. I passed one of my former Navy divert bases from when I was on an aircraft carrier in the Indian Ocean. I thought I was seeing some really remote areas. Think again.

The next day, after a preparatory meeting with the local military, we convoyed to about as far as you can get in that country. I was riding with a Brit who worked for the current representative as the chief engineer / program manager. He had done this for years in the region. The sand dunes were spectacular. I asked how the occasional bush stayed put. "It doesn't. Moves with the dunes." I asked about the water ponds I saw here and there. "Artisan wells. Below the bedrock is a lot of water. It just can't get out." I saw them building a road to nowhere with tiny bulldozers in the distance. "They are not tiny. They are just a long way off, moving a huge dune."

I asked about the security situation. He said the first six months on the job, they had seven Land Rovers hijacked at gunpoint. He himself was almost nabbed but went at full speed straight across the desert to escape. They asked for government security and got it; several intruders were *eliminated* one night outside their compound. The local military commander then invited him in for a meeting and suggested he meet with the local hetman and see if a relationship couldn't be established to prevent further eliminations. He did. Of course, the local hetman spoke no English, and he spoke very little Arabic. But with a translator and some tea, they got to the point where the hetman suggested kindly that the local kids could use a schoolbag. Bingo—twenty schoolbags with notebooks, pencils, pens, crayons— anything a local kid could need in elementary school. Next weekly meeting—boy, sure would be convenient for the teachers if they could copy their stuff easily. Bingo—copy/printer with paper and ink for a year. You can take this along. Each week a request, and the company paid, and no more gunpoint SUV requisitions.

Moral: In international business, you need to understand the local environment and identify the local needs before just plowing into the situation. Sometimes the solution is simple, inexpensive, and extremely effective.

Other items should really not bear mentioning, but I will. Try to learn your local area. Look for multiple routes out—out of the hotel, out of an intersection, and out of a mall that you shop in frequently. Keep your mobile phone fully charged. This can be a challenge, but I cannot count the times I have had my company brethren and sisters show up begging for a charge line for their phone. Stick with reputable taxis. Most places have them well marked. But even I pulled a rookie mistake on one of my first visits to Saudi Arabia. I picked what looked like a real taxi, only to have another gent climb in the front seat as we took off and to have the driver stop and take off the taxi sign from the roof once out of the airport. It seems he was really just picking up a friend and used me to pay the gas. From then on, I either had my representative, my local employee, or the hotel meet me with a sign. Keep all your paperwork, medicines, and glasses on you or in your airplane carry-on. You don't want to arrive missing them. Do check the web for good checklists. They are usually a somber read, but at least you get to thinking.

Now, Finland was hardly a security issue. Clean, organized, well patrolled. Even the local citizens would tsk-tsk you if you jaywalked an otherwise empty street to save walking down to the crosswalk and back. Your biggest security issue was the cold that it could be in the winter. Fortunately, the hotels and offices were warm and cozy. This allowed me to focus on issues other than my safety.

It was during my time on the Finland program that I began to learn about some of the other aspects of international business. The first is the export control regime of the US government. As this program was technically a government-to-government deal, we had it easy in terms of transferring data and equipment. I would pass it to my USG counterpart for review, and then he would either pass it on or send a note saying, "Go for it." In the defense and high-technology industries, though, export is a big deal. I spent most of my life working inside the International Traffic in Arms Regulations (ITAR), and not all of it has been as smooth as it was with Finland. Though it came later in my career, it is also important to note that ITAR is not the only export regime of the USG. There is also the Department of Commerce's Export Administration Regulations (EAR) as well as several lists of sanctions and denied parties, such as the Treasury Department's Office of Foreign Assets Control (OFAC). It is this complex picture of getting both goods and services out of the US that leads to my recommendation: get some training in it.

ITAR is controlled by the Department of State. It takes its review inputs from all services and many other agencies, but it has the final determination. This can lead to issues when, for instance, the Department of Defense wants partners for an international program, while the State Department worries about the leakage of technology. ITAR violations carry the largest fines. State does investigations and makes sure of its footing before taking action. Therefore, while the fines are large—tens of millions recently—they are fewer per year—say three or four. Many of the cases actually start when a company realizes it has violated ITAR inadvertently. Self-reporting and assisting with the investigation help reduce the penalty, but for major infractions, a penalty still comes along.

What to Do in the South of Spain

Fast-forward two decades and several companies later, and there I was ... on a company-paid vacation to the south of Spain. Technically, it was our annual business-development group hug. And those events are, in fact, hugely important for internal networking. That started with a golf game the previous day with a colleague who I didn't get to see too often (he won).

Anyway, we were at the gala dinner midweek when my cell phone rang. I recognized the number and stepped out to take the call (24/7/365 generally characterized this particular job assignment). Our export folks were calling in a panic to say improper equipment had been shipped to my region (Middle East), and could I get it back *now*. So now I stepped back in and flagged over a couple of my guys to listen to the conversation, including one of the representatives from the destination country who had been invited to attend the conference. We were a thousand miles away, and the shipment had landed. There was no way we were going to intervene before the weekend at best.

Rest of the story: The local customer was the air

force. They were expecting a certain number of items. Quantity was perfect, but the type was not. Of course, they opened all the boxes for a quality check. On realizing what was up, they said merely that they would keep the items safe until the proper ones arrived. But per US export regulations, we were out of export limits by quantity and had to get a new license to ship the remainder, even though they were the proper items. This the export staff did in record time. We did get back the improperly shipped items, but it did result in increased scrutiny of my company's export practices. I never did hear where the actual shipping mistake was made.

Moral: As the outpost of the company, your job as an international business person relies heavily on a team back home. Work closely with them, and hopefully you won't have to help in these unfortunate situations.

Back in the day of the far-flung British Empire, an expatriate based months away overseas could—and often did—get away with daring, even occasionally egregious, use of their nominal powers. The expansion of British influence via the East India Company in the Indian subcontinent comes to mind as the perfect example of aggressive leaders making deals with local princes, fighting and winning battles and new provinces—all months away from getting permission, making acquisitions there and elsewhere basically a fait accompli. Not so much in today's digitally connected world, although as the expat representative of your company, you often do have a lot of independence of decision and action, which is one reason companies try hard to pick good expatriates and keep the ones they have that are trusted on-station and on the payroll. With my first boss in Malaysia, we reached a deal even before I moved. He promised to read every email and listen to any voice mails I left over the course of a day. All he asked was that they be short and have a recommended action plan that I could execute. If he did not reply, I had automatic permission to go ahead with my plan. This helped a lot with working on training, logistics, and the occasional party planning. By the time I was in the Middle East, the digital world and improved communication also had gotten more cost-effective. In this case, the company also had a formalized, online delegation of decision and cost authority. While I always kept the boss in the know, if I needed something done immediately—demo equipment parts, fixtures for our test equipment, and so on—as long as it was under my limit, I just did it and let my enterprising engineers find the best local business entity and get it done.

Speaking of 24/7/365, be aware that international business will try your endurance as well as your time zone calculations. Of course, the explosion of computers and handheld devices now makes it easier to stay in touch anywhere and anytime. But it doesn't make that midnight or one-in-the-morning call any more inviting. For Finland, I would go in early to have a several-hour overlap with my counterparts in Finland. In Malaysia, email was getting more prevalent. I was twelve hours out of sync with the head office. My boss was good about sending a short note when he wanted to chat and vice versa. However, I had another colleague who never quite got that down and would call for a long chat at around ten thirty at night my time. While in my globe-trotting stage, I was asked to join a small subgroup of a business-oriented nongovernmental organization—of which my company was a member—while they rewrote their charter. That was fine and a good experience, except most of them were in Washington, DC, while my travels took me frequently to Korea and Turkey, so the telecons were often at two in the morning. In the Middle East, I also had a very understanding boss who got into the habit of checking in while he drove to work early in the morning his time—late afternoon mine.

Vacations. Another issue. Every culture has its own vacation cycle. If you are an internationalist, you need to be attuned to the local vacations. For instance, Australia's summer is in the North American winter. There is some overlap with the Christmas and New Year's holiday period but not nearly enough. For the Muslim world, you need to track and avoid the post–Ramadan Eid holidays, and the Hajj holiday that follows a month or so later, as well as a few extras here and there. For Nordic Europe, forget about work during July and late June. For much of Europe, July and August are meagre pickings for setting up business meetings. Sure, Canada has aligned its Thanksgiving with the US version, but not many Brits take off the Fourth of July weekend. And of course few countries have overlapping independence days or king's birthdays. You have to, as an international businessperson, adapt to their holidays. Outlook, smartphones, and other calendars can help now, of course, especially if you are focused on just one or two countries. But the number of notifications starts getting crazy if your market is a dozen or more countries. This will lead to friction when your boss wants a deal sealed *now*, yet now is the beginning or middle of a major local holiday. If you are an expatriate, you may reap the benefits of both holidays; your company is shut down while you are technically supposed to work, and the country is shut down while your company wants you to work. But in the end, you still have to try to make deals happen, support the customer, and otherwise flog on.

A final time theme note: daylight saving time changes—I grew to detest them. First, the countries around the world do not share a common date for the switch. You really do need a web app like TimeTrader or WorldTimeServer to keep up with all the changes. And, of course, many countries in the tropics never bother changing. It could be a real pain, especially for routinely scheduled calls. And it was even worse when those on the calls were in three different regions of the world—practically guaranteeing that at DST switchover points, regular meetings would get messed up or missed.

I return to ITAR and exporting. ITAR is not an area you can "just do it." In my experience, it has gotten more formal over the years, as well as more restrictive, but also more digital. What often used to take a year can sometimes now be adjudicated by the USG in a month or two. ITAR reviews remain a very formulized process. Large companies will have individuals certified by the USG to sign a license submittal that everything is correct. Once into the system, State will start the review process and route the request to appropriate multiple USG agencies (commonly Defense, for instance, who farms it out to the appropriate service). There is an online tracking system for a lot of this; your designated representative can track progress. Stated target is ninety days, but I have experienced complicated cases taking a year. Trade shows can be a special case, but you still have to have the temporary export approval. This can lead to some stress, both in getting the license and in executing the show. Vigilance is a must.

Missing Equipment

There I was … commiserating with my boss on an incident at an international trade show.

Turns out that a piece of equipment had gone missing. It was a thermal sniper scope. This from a display stand fully staffed by a number of company employees. Unbelievable as it was, my boss was being accused of having stolen it to sell on the black market. That particular innuendo was internal company politics and sniping between different power-hungry groups. But everything that could have been done had been done. The loss was immediately reported to the local police. Forms were filled. Future shows would see the equipment literally chained down to prevent five-fingered thefts.

Enter the local hero.

One of the policemen that had lodged the report had a hunting hobby. The weekend after the show, he was surfing on his own time a hunter-focused equipment sales website. Lo and behold, up pops this thermal sniper scope—"perfect for plugging animals at night." He didn't take more than a couple of seconds to put two and two together and with his department worked up a sting operation to purchase the sight—and arrest the thief, who attempted to lie that he just randomly found the sight in a garbage bin. A quick search of his cell phone's travels over the previous week showed the gent clearly at the trade show the entire day of the theft. Thank you, Mr. Policeman!

Moral: If you are selling pilferable items, better lock them down with cables or chains, especially if they are ITAR controlled. You cannot be everywhere all the time, and it takes only seconds to make off with expensive kit.

One of the hardest items is to get through an exemption to national disclosure policy. This is a very tight needle to crawl through, sometimes even for close allies as potential customers. Keep in mind that you have to have a marketing license even to approach a government with the product. After you make a sale, you then have to return for the actual export license, which means a second chance for the USG to change its mind. I once had a marketing license returned approved, and I didn't believe it. It was sensitive technology, and though to a close ally, I chose to request a meeting with a portion of the review committee. Sure enough, this license had "slipped through the cracks and been approved." Their words. I asked my chances on getting permission to actually export the hardware in the near future. "None."

Why "Hey, Not My fault" Doesn't Work in Offset

A Joint Strike Fighter (JSF/F-35) Story, the Names Changed to Protect Both the Innocent and the Guilty
There I was … dual-hatted business development and offset. (That seems to happen to me a lot. Even knowing how to spell offset correctly gets you the job sometimes.)
I was in a country attempting to set up the industrial participation framework for a large platform. I was the major subcontractor to the major prime, and my prime's offset colleague had asked me to accompany him on visits specifically to help me and my company congeal some real offset arrangements.
To reiterate, I was working on Platform-System B for Big, not F for JSF/F-35.
We walked into the local conference room of a major international company and were joined by a dozen of their staff. We were outnumbered three or four to one. After handshakes and business card exchanges, the opening salvo …
"Why is your company refusing to give us work on the F-35?" Whoa—not only "not my fault" but "not my

job (i.e., program)." Of course, you absolutely cannot say these things—at least more than once. Over the course of a two-hour meeting, I got to take full shots in the face for upward of ninety minutes from a very upset major industry player, because (root cause) US export determinations had not allowed my company's part of the JSF program to issue viable requests for proposals and, in fact, had been designed to attempt to limit any foreign participation in what was at that point a seven-country collaborative development. Work—very significant work, in fact—had already been allocated to this country *and* this company, but that was a different division, whose divisional representative in this particular meeting said absolutely nothing and sipped his coffee without making eye contact.

The thirty minutes we did spend on my project yielded some good follow-up investigations and discussions.

As we were heading back to the hotel, my prime counterpart had the pity and decency to say that: a) he had no idea that was coming; and b) he thought I had handled that in as an exemplary manner as was possible given the hostile situation.

Moral: If your company has more than one iron in a particular country's campfire, make sure you connect with your counterparts on a routine basis to know where the points of pain are located, or you and your program get to wear the brand.

The Department of State is not the only export controller in the US. The Department of Commerce gets everything not considered critical military technology. These fall under the Export Administration Regulations (EAR). There is still paperwork associated with EAR license requests and tracking, but it is far less onerous. For instance, for ITAR, you need to get an end user receipt acknowledgment. For EAR, Commerce is satisfied with just the intermediary—as if you are selling a product or service to a middleman or representative to then sell onward on your behalf. At any rate, much like ITAR, EAR has sections detailing what is covered by Commerce and what is needed to allow it to be exported. They do have a large catch-all category for items clearly not needing tracking. The best is to ask. All USG departments will accept a letter called a General Correspondence. In this letter, you can ask for a pre–license application determination on your chances of getting permission to export. While not binding, the review process is quicker, and you get a general feel for what might happen, thereby saving time and money. But the basic message is that just because you are operating in the civilian market does not mean you have no need to pay attention to export regulations. Commerce is just as serious about violations; they file many more claims each year than State—just smaller fines.

Check the Address

There I was … listening to the tribulations of some of my colleagues as we all received our annual export training. Turns out our company had to report itself on an incorrect export shipment. It seemed a little unfair, but lessons were learned, so here is the tale.

As part of its commercial expansion into China, the company was partnering with a Chinese company up in northern China for parts. To facilitate this, our company was taking excess machining equipment from a US plant it was closing and shipping it to the facility in China. All this had been thoroughly vetted with the USG, as the machining tools, while not new, had very high capability. The license stipulated they were all to go to the new joint venture facility for use on civil transport parts.

Enter a partner manager. He correctly pointed out that as soon as the equipment hit China, the level of English would be low, and all the crates really should be marked with a Chinese-script address as well. This sounded very logical, and our company tasked the engineer to do the translation. Off the crates went. And then, some months after, we began to wonder why the machine tools had not shown up at the facility. After getting a little bit of a runaround from the partner and the government, our company finally hired its own translator to read the characters that had been painted on the box. Turns out the characters in the stencil were the address to a government military plant in far western China.

We self-reported, and the USG stepped in and got the Chinese to ship the tools to where they were supposed to go. Even so, our company had to pay a fine as well as enter a compliance agreement, one stipulation of which, if I understand correctly, was to have all addresses translated by an independent translator before items shipped overseas.

> Moral: Even large companies with well-staffed export departments can make honest mistakes, but in international and controlled transactions, the government will still take a relatively dim view of the subject. Check and double-check in the ITAR-controlled environment.

The final major department is the Treasury Department's Office of Foreign Asset Control (OFAC). OFAC is a money transfer / investment-oriented regulation that focuses more on specific countries, companies, and even people who the USG doesn't trust and doesn't want American companies doing business with. They do keep databases that are searchable, but probably a letter is easiest if you are not an expert. I know they also respond to emails now—something for your Pearl Harbor file, though remember the USG can take a dim view: ignorance of the law is no excuse.

Back to Finland. In addition to coming up a steep learning curve on the proper way to handle ITAR exports, I was also being gradually introduced to a concept called offsets. I will cover offsets in some detail in a couple of chapters, but for here, suffice it to say it is a form of countertrade, industrial participation, localization, and various other phrases placing work or investment into country as part of a quid pro quo for having bought your product. My colleague doing the offsets would from time to time ask for ideas or support. One of these came along in a peculiar manner.

The Finns were very proud to be acquiring the F-18. A local artist wanted to make a statue of an F-18 out of concrete for a park in Helsinki. By helping the artist, we could get a little bit of offset credit. So, my offset colleague asked me if I could figure out how to get the outside mold line or aircraft shape for the artist. I checked around with the structural engineers. Sure enough, they had the aircraft's shape on a series of computer files. It sounded highly technical, but I was assured by the engineers that the files were old; we no longer used them and had upgraded to a different system. And the file matches were only approximate; it was most certainly good enough for pouring a concrete statue but not for real detailed engineering. With that story, I got the disk exported via the USG to the Finnish Air Force, and Helsinki got its concrete F-18 statue. The rest of this story is that some time later I was talking with the senior Finnish engineer, and out of the blue, he thanked me profusely (well, as profusely as Finns can, which is low-key and usually in a sauna) for that data. I asked why, and he said they had patiently matched up all files so that they really did now have a nice mold line model. Fortunately, we can trust the Finns to keep it safer than we do. But, technically, I missed a huge potential offset in technology transfer (don't tell my colleague).

This does raise a good point. One of the reasons countries may have offsets (covered in chapter 4) is to try to lower the hurdle for acquiring advanced technologies. In many cases—direct sales or offsets—the company ends up being the unpaid advocate for a country to ratchet up the technology ladder. This is due to the company's ability as a taxpaying member of the US to justify why a particular technology or capability should be released under export regulations. The simplest method is to demonstrate to the USG's satisfaction that the restricted technology is already available from other, non-US sources, and a US export restriction is impeding exports from the US in favor of other countries' exports. It gets harder after that, but sometimes you can rely on alliances to justify a release, such as the ability of a country to invest in a joint overseas operation, and the commonality of the equipment helps both the US economy (your company) and the US soldier (deployed close to the subject country). Of course, there are always bounds, and sometimes alliances change.

Transfer without License

There I was … some years later, learning ever more about exports and ITAR and how to appropriately handle odd questions. When you do international business, especially in the defense business, you do get some interesting contacts.

My first was while I was assigned to Southeast Asia, and it came via a third party that wanted to set me up with Vietnam to sell F-15s. I immediately reported this to the US embassy military attaché in Hanoi. The response was not what I expected; I got an interesting chuckle from the embassy. "Well, they could afford them, but that won't happen." Next contact, perhaps a year or so later—CH-47s. US embassy response: "We could really use some updated helicopters for recovery of Vietnam War–era US military remains. We just had a crash with a team traveling in an old Soviet-era chopper that cost us a couple US military lives." I don't think that happened until years later, but obviously Vietnam and US relationships had improved.

Forward a number of years to another region with decidedly shadier characters. I got an email contact for some tower-mounted cameras in Iraq. The exchange started politely enough. I knew we sold some after the second US invasion and before their terrible civil war, so a follow-on order, especially for oil field surveillance, was not a surprise. But the equipment at that time was ITAR controlled, so certain protocols had to be followed. I provided the formats for end user certificates to be filled and returned so I could process export licenses. This is when the emails became, well, odd. I was asked a couple of times if the forms were necessary. I replied yes. Then I got the terminating email: "Our customer is willing to make it personally worth your while to not have to fill in these forms, and to have you do them." Took about fifteen seconds for me to send a termination "do not contact me again" note, and another couple minutes to forward the note to my legal staff so these guys could not end-run us through some perhaps less reputable representatives or staff in the region.

Moral: Without fail, in international business you will be asked to cross a thin line from time to time on a variety of topics—export regulations included. Don't do it.

The banner recent example was the export of the then-new F-14 Tomcat to Iran while the Shah was in charge. A few years later, the Shaw was disposed, and a regime inimical to the US had those top-line fighters, either for their own use or to transfer to their newfound best friends, the Soviet Union.

Culturally, I enjoyed the Finns a lot. I made more noise in a meeting than their entire staff. But they seemed to enjoy being around someone who was a bit rambunctious. They also appreciated my staying in the program so long. I think in the five years I was on the program, I had at least three, and maybe four, USG counterparts, but none of my Finnish counterparts changed. I became the one constant they could rely on (at least in the engineering area). We did quite a bit, from touring their bases and facilities to learning how to do a true Finnish sauna. I did a lot of snow jumping but only went into a frozen lake through a hole in the ice once (survived).

Going to the Bar Naked

There I was … going to a bar naked—the things you do in international business.

We were in the first major in-country program-management review with a large number of contractor and USG personnel. The customer was putting their best foot forward. A dinner was hosted at the local officers' club, where the prime feature was to be a local sauna. We all piled into the bar while the food was being prepared. Because of the number of folks, we had to go to the sauna in shifts (the sauna there holding maybe ten to twelve folks comfortably). I got invited to the first shift.

Now, locally, the tradition is to steam yourself like a lobster, then go jump in a lake (preferably frozen). But with no lake close by, the alternate tradition is to throw yourself into the snow. At this particular club, the third tradition was to climb out through the small sauna window (that is, through the snow) and, after cooling, walk into the bar for a club-sponsored schnapps and return to the sauna. Oh, saunas are done naked.

I heard this story while in the sauna. I didn't believe it. They tried to goad me that the competitors had done it, but I pointed out the competitors lost. However, they then said the USAF had done it. As a Navy guy, this becomes a point of pride. I climbed out the window buck naked, dug through the snow pile, and strolled into the bar that previously was filled to the brim with people. Fortunately, the buffet had just opened, and no one was there. As I walked to the bar, the burly-looking barmaid carefully but oh so slowly pulled up a shot glass and poured a schnapps. I slugged it down, then strolled out as one of my colleagues came running in with the fig leaf pose over his privates. As soon as I got back to the sauna, I verified the story—and everyone else went out the window.

After dressing, I went up to the buffet. One of the ladies there grabbed me and whispered, "I think naked people are going to the bar!" I quickly explained the tradition, and an evil grin covered her face. Next thing we knew, there was a line of chairs from the bar entrance to the bar, with the ladies sitting in them with their food and drinks, taking pictures of the naked guys going to the bar! Even the ladies (when it was their turn to sauna) did their bit, though they did wear wrapped towels.

Fast-forward a couple of weeks. Context: Tailhook 1991 (a year or so prior). Huge sexual harassment event and internal navy discipline action. Someone at this program-management event had forwarded the program evening's proceedings to the navy's judge advocate general. Our lawyers called us all in for a discussion. For us, no harm, no foul. But some of our Navy brethren could be in for stormy weather. We all disavowed seeing any USG personnel participate, which is all our lawyers wanted to hear.

The issue was fixed by the heroics of the Navy's naval attaché in country. He was called into a buddy's office on a trip to DC. After some socializing remarks, this guy came to the point. Did it happen? The attaché's response: "Yes, and if you have an issue with it, you have no business doing business in this country. I have a certificate signed by the chief of their air force that said I did this sauna the full nine yards." That apparently turned the tide. The attaché produced the duly signed certificate (we all got one), and all charges and investigations ceased. The country did get a polite but pointed note from the Navy asking them to neither send nor encourage Americans to go to the bar naked.

Postscript: The story, of course, grew in the telling. As my USG colleagues rotated, I had a new, fiery individual who heard about it and wanted to try. But on our first trip together in-country, our host indicated, to my colleague's great disappointment, that the interior window handle had been removed so we Americans wouldn't go out it. About eighteen months later, I was there on an introductory trip for my replacement, again with my USG colleague. We were in the sauna joking about the situation. The host said, "Oh, we forgot to remove the handle this time." My USG colleague was out the window in a heartbeat (yes, followed by the rest of us) ... but this time no tattletales.

Moral: Some cultural experiences may put you into an uncomfortable zone. In today's business age, you usually can ask for an out, but you will miss out on a closer bond with your customer.

Not all Finnish saunas end that way, by the way. This was very location specific. But I tremendously enjoyed my time with the Finns. They had wanted me to consider moving to Finland as the next in-country manager—something that might have occurred, except for a new opportunity that popped up practically out of nowhere.

I loved the Finns, their history, their culture, and their ability to make a decisive decision when required. Personally, they were quiet but friendly. Even in the hotel gym, if there was only one there, they would smile and practice their English on me, though in public they'd be a bit shier. One gent in the gym struck up quite the conversation as we swapped workout machines and traded a little personal background. I finally complimented his English and asked if he had been to the US. "No." To the UK, then, for an extended period? "No." Was his background in international business? No, he was a car dealer, strictly in Finland. A bit bewildered, I said the English-language training in the Finnish public school system must be outstanding. He shook his head. I finally asked where the heck he had learned such good English. Wait for it ... MTV!

Anyway, the Finns and this program helped me grow tremendously in the international business arena in many aspects: export, offset, and the definition of "technical neutrality" that often hovered on the edges of both their policies and the policies of other countries that I was to deal with.

Around the World while spinning dizzily and getting yanked back and forth like a yo-yo—expatriate life in international business.

CHAPTER 3

Digging Deeper into International Business
Different Cultures, Life as an Expatriate, Financial Crisis

Remember that "Wrong" at the end of chapter 1? Well, here it comes. I was fat dumb and happy working the Finland program when into my little cubbyhole bounced my counterpart on the Malaysian F/A-18 Program. He was having a good chuckle. It seemed that the in-country program manager for that program was going to be replaced. The overall program manager was in a quandary. He felt he needed a person strong on the technical side of the F/A-18, familiar with military logistics, a thorough understanding of the USN international staff, structure, and rules, and ideally with some military operational experience to help the country absorb the new fighter. My buddy then chuckles and leaves, saying, "No one could possibly meet all those criteria!" But as Bill Murray says in *Groundhog Day*, "Me, me, me, also me": nine years working technical issues on the F/A-18, four of them closely with the Navy's international office, and seven years as a Navy fighter pilot, usually with a day job as a maintenance division officer. And I had worked for several years with the program director of the Malaysian program while he had been on the Finland program before he moved to take over his current position, so he knew me quite well.

I decided to pop over to that boss's office, poke my head in, and basically volunteer to be considered. I told my wife about the potential that night. Her only comment was, "I didn't get to finish my shopping there when the wives stayed in Kuala Lumpur overnight on the way to meet you guys in Perth." Ugh—not a good sign. A few days later, the potential boss stopped by and said I was certainly on the list, but they would have to do the usual internal posting, so it would take a while. About a month after that, I got called down to the vice president's office. He said, "Well, this really isn't the proper way to go about this, but we all decided you are the perfect fit, and we will just give you the job. Please don't tell anyone, though, as we skipped a bunch of human resources steps."

Malaysia is a delightful country. During my years there, it was generally one of great growth, except for the 1997–1998 currency crisis. It was a trading entrepot since practically before recorded time. Starting with the Portuguese in the 1500s, those entrepots began to change European hands about every century as the Dutch followed the Portuguese and the Brits followed the Dutch. The Brits had a huge local impact by importing workers from both India and China. Getting its independence in 1957, Malaysia has done well with only a few bumps in the road—one unfortunately occurring while I was there with the 1997–1998 worldwide currency crisis.

The financial crisis of 1997–1998 in Southeast Asia does raise one issue of being devoted to international business: many factors are largely out of your control. This occurred in Malaysia just as I was transitioning from program management to business development. On the program side, I had a single focus—help the Malaysian air force properly support their new aircraft. This was a national-priority program and would remain relatively insulated from the crisis. However, in business development, I was to sell more stuff—fighters, helicopters, weapons, and so on. And not just to Malaysia. I inherited Thailand and Brunei and was to help my boss in Singapore and in Indonesia. All these economies ground to a halt and went on the defensive to recover from the currency-related crisis of those years. I made calls, office calls, presentations, helped with air shows—all with nothing to show for it. That is one reason I did my second master's during that period—both a faint hope of better networking and a way to fill the day when the phone just didn't ring all that often. In the end, my lack of performance was noted, and it was decided to replace me. (My replacement didn't sell large program in the intervening years either.)

I am not an economics expert, so I will not delve into the causes and cures for this crisis. There are several books on it for the interested reader. However, I will relate my experiences. In addition to the impact it had on my ability to develop my line of business, I saw numerous other effects of the downturn. The most visually dramatic was the halt in all the construction in the region. The standing joke when I arrived was that the national bird of Malaysia was the Building Crane. But in 1997, the Building Cranes abruptly stopped breeding. A major complex on my drive to work halted at about the twentieth floor—and as we left four years later, not a thing had progressed. A monorail public transportation system was stopped in midwork, leaving a line of Stonehenge-like monoliths through the downtown (on my return for business a decade later, it was finished and running). A huge four-story mansion just up the road from our condominium complex, a property of the brother of the Sultan of Brunei, also stopped in midwork. After a couple of years, we saw the local homeless men gradually dismantling the metal scaffolds and hauling them by twos and threes past our condo to some unknown location in the near downtown—obviously selling them for scrap. It was disconcerting to watch, as they were taking the scaffolds apart from the bottom up! When we did finally leave, the abandoned concrete edifice was still there, but not a bit of the metal scaffold.

On the personal side, the first year or so in our condo complex had been a nice mix of European, Australian, and Asian families. None of my kids' closest friends were American, and the American-curriculum expatriate school they went to had only about 25 percent of the kids from the US (the next largest being Sweden). But as the crisis unfolded, droves of these expats left. Our nice Italian next-door neighbor went back to Italy. My kids' closest friends from Korea and Australia returned home. The school itself had to deal with the decline in enrollment and wrestle with staffing and budgets. The return of the expats was only just beginning as we departed in 2002. This crimped our social life, and as the newcomers arrived, we welcomed them, but it was harder to integrate, as the traditions and fabric of the expatriate community had been torn.

For the locals, the downturn was traumatic on multiple fronts. For my government counterparts, there were wage freezes and retirement-age extensions. Nongovernment sectors saw layoffs, and hiring was frozen. I, my local associate, and my visitors saw this in the downtown traffic. What had usually been a miserable slug in the rush hour was now almost speed-limit driving; my commute home went from forty-five minutes to about twenty for many months. Fewer cars, more parking spots. I had an interesting conversation with a taxi driver who had excellent English. He was back driving a cab after his firm downsized. He was miserable at his losses in the local bourse. It was interesting to hear him discuss the stock exchange, as he had almost treated it as legalized gambling. He was leveraged and trading almost daily. The local exchange had dropped almost 80 percent in eighteen months, and he was one of those wiped out. The exchange rate benefited us as expats but not many of the locals unless they were working for a large international firm. But the country doggedly pressed on, with a noteworthy performance hosting the Commonwealth Games in the middle of the crisis in 1998. This was all the more impressive since, in addition to all the new sports venues built, they inaugurated their first nontrain public rail transportation—elevated and underground mass transit. My family traveled by the new rail system to watch several of the events—delightful! In any event, this was not my only brush with economic downturns and their impact on being an international businessman. Later in my career, I had the distinct displeasure of two more crises, which I will briefly cover later in the book.

This is a great time to discuss expatriate life. Allow me a moderate digression to cover all three of our overseas assignments, including experiences with housing and cars, shopping, mailing, banking, taxation policies, and overall expat packages. Going abroad as an expatriate is the ultimate international experience. I do not mean life in the Peace Corps, of course (though I know from some of my kids' friends that that is also quite the positive experience). At the corporate level, you have many things to consider. First, your family. How will they take it, and how will they approach the new situations they will encounter overseas? When I announced to my wife the possibility of going to Malaysia, she was all for it, and the kids at six and nine years of age didn't have much of a vote. For the company, though, this is an expensive proposition. Packages usually include appropriate housing and cost of living allowances. There is an entire industry built up to support expatriate assignments, and often the allowances provided are based on the data (gotten from somewhere—I have no idea where) on what other companies are doing for their expats at a similar level of management or skill set. If, like me, you are closely aligned with USG contracts, then what the government policy is will also bear on your package. Note that "appropriate" housing carries many connotations, many of them based on cost. What you as an American think is appropriate may not be what the company wants to afford. Many countries have different standards, often with smaller abodes and lack of central heat and air-conditioning being two that I routinely have seen. It is part of the adventure, for sure, but it may be an uncomfortable part if the family is not on board with the adventure.

Cars are generally an issue. First off, it is 99 percent likely that it is singular—one car. If you are heading over with a spouse, you will need to address that point. Some places have secondhand cars for a reasonable cost; others, not so much. I would leave the vehicle while on business trips—in Malaysia, for instance, usually once a week. That allowed my wife to get the groceries home without arriving bathed in sweat and with melted ice cream. There may be an option to ship your personal car. If so, plan on a wait measured in months in a rental. And keep in mind that for the substantial portion of the world that drives on the left side of the road (e.g., UK), you will be at a disadvantage in many driving situations.

Paid schooling for the kids is relatively standard, especially in countries where the base language of instruction is not (for an American) English. This is a huge cost, though, as these are always private schools. Vacations to return home once a year are also often included. Sometimes the company will toss in the travel time as an extra vacation day, sometimes not. But when you are a day's flight away each direction, that day is a help.

Will your furniture ship with you or go into storage? If not shipping your personal effects, the company should offer an allowance to outfit the rental in the foreign location. A good boss will drive a hard bargain but relent once you use up all the funds for reasonable furniture and are still short. Otherwise, it will be on you. Buying locally available items is generally a good idea for another reason: if, heaven forbid, you have to flee the country due to a local disturbance or a natural disaster, you should be less attached to the quick-bought stuff than your own household goods back in the States. Unless, of course, like my wife, you have plunged into buying as much rosewood as you can afford (and then some). Oh well—that is also one of the perks of living overseas.

You may be evacuated for periods of time, either voluntarily or mandatory. In our case, we were given the option while in Southeast Asia for a voluntary family evacuation in 1997 due to the heavy smoke from forest fires blanketing the area. We literally could not see anything but a very weak sun at midday, and horizontal visibility was well under a mile. We all had heavy-duty painters' masks (the ones with the canisters attached, not the simple paper ones you cover your mouth with) for when we were outside—not fun to jog in (I now see at the gym some kind of mask to make breathing harder for training swimmers while they exercise out of the water). We chose not to send everyone home; instead, I was given permission to use the allocated funds to fly us for a week's break out of the smog. We went instead to the Maldives—a diving and beach location with stunningly clear water and abundant reef life that was a great break from the routine. Check out the island resort Bandos! Others, though, sent the spouse and kids back to live with relatives in the home country for several months, making the continuity of schooling an issue. Your choice, based on company policy and the local circumstances.

Groceries. You are going to need to cook and eat. And, in spite of the wonderful local foods, you will quickly long for your staples from the homeland: cereal in the morning, sandwiches midday, and steaks or fried chicken at night. I ignore in this statement a colleague who had to can his own vegetables that they personally grew in their backyard while on an extended assignment in a Southwest Asian country due to health concerns from the local produce. In Kuala Lumpur during my time, it was not nearly so difficult. However, there was exactly one place to go to get American stuff. I believe it was called the Ampang Grocer. It had Cheerios, pretzels, the brands of snack and junk food our kids were used to, peanut butter, and sometimes my daughter's favorite, white cheddar cheese popcorn, and ... bacon!

Yes, twice I have lived in a Muslim country. While neither country forbade pork products, they were difficult to come by. In Malaysia with its large Chinese minority, most Chinese shops would carry something, but it didn't look like what we were used to in the US. But the Ampang Grocer carried Oscar Mayer. In the Middle East, certain stores had a carefully separated and clearly marked Not Halal section with pork products—not only bacon but pepperoni for pizzas, ribs for barbeque, and so on. In Malaysia, with growing kids, we would make a trek once a month across town to the one grocery store with US products and fill the car to overflowing. To be frank, we did find that a pain and gradually accommodated many tastes to the very large selection of available British origin snacks and spreads. The very large UK and Australian population made those worthwhile to stock in most stores. But the US products only crept in very slowly and in small doses.

By the time I was in the Middle East about a decade later, I found far more US products permeating the major local grocery stores. The apartment I picked was partially chosen precisely because it was by a huge, big-box store equivalent in an adjoining mall, not to mention all the other mall stores—some standard international brands and some locally unique. I could just walk over, although those 120 steps between air-conditioning in the summer months would still leave me absolutely soaked with sweat on returning to the apartment. Over my five years there, more and more US-origin (or design—probably local or regional origin) products began to appear on its shelves, including—miracle of miracles one day—Dr. Pepper, and occasionally Diet Dr. Pepper! I gradually stopped going to the one store that had a larger selection of US products as well as the pork, as I was trying to cut down on the fat anyway, and my next-door supermarket now had 95 percent of what I had originally driven across town to buy. Also, one of my colleagues who stayed with me for a couple of weeks during a local move found and ate all my stored bacon while I was on a business trip. Humpf. (Payback was his girlfriend cooking a delightful salmon steak one night and a surreptitiously abandoned bottle of full gin when he moved on.)

The key to this kind of survival was always networking. As I chatted with other expat friends and colleagues, I would learn of the specific advantages and products in various stores throughout the city (in both Malaysia and the Middle East) and be able to broaden my shopping options. In both locations, my family was within a relatively easy (if hot) walk to the mall, giving options when there was no car for the wife or when traffic was so bad you didn't want to fight it. So, in selecting your overseas domicile, walk a couple of blocks in all directions to see what is convenient. Our doctor in Malaysia—who I credit with saving my life once—was also within a walk. Good thing for when my wife drove me there terribly ill and couldn't find parking.

Malaysian Fruit

There I was … back in Penang again but this time with the family, early in our tour there, for their first look at the island and city. I was using Eddie, the driver I had started to use for work on my routine trips, and he gave us the grand tour. He drove us completely around the island's perimeter road, then hit the downtown architecture and market and the tramway up the local mountain—all great!

Part of that tour was a stop at a local roadside fruit stand for us to sample fruits that were foreign to us. Three stuck out in particular. The first was the rambutan, a smallish, hairy red fruit about the size of a small tangerine with a sweet, white core. You opened it by twisting it hard. The second was the mangosteen—a purple-colored fruit also with a sweet white core. Its caution was that it would stain your clothes purple if you were messy. Both of these all the family at least attempted to try.

But the final one was the durian—practically the national fruit of Malaysia. It must have been one really hungry ancestor that first tried it. It has a hard outer skin covered with small spikes. You had to open it using gloves and a machete. While the size of a melon, the only edible part was in the core, and that didn't look much meatier than the small rambutan. But—let me tell you—a durian stinks to high heaven! Imagine wet, stinky athletic socks, and you are almost there. You saw signs in hotel lobbies and in taxis saying, No Durian Allowed. There are hundreds of varieties, and they are carefully guarded by their owners so they aren't stolen during the season. Large nets are spread to catch them as they fall or are knocked off the tree. I was the only one in the family brave enough to get past the smell for a taste. I thought the best description I could come up with was "like vanilla ice cream with onion sauce." You are either a durian lover or a durian hater, and I came down squarely in the latter category. Even among the locals, you had a few that were not fans; one colleague said he was the only one in his family who did not like durian. He would have to flee the house when all the others got ready to open up a few for a durian feast. I tasted that durian flavor well past dinner, and I am lucky my wife didn't kick me out of bed for the night.

Moral: There are many things you get to learn and try when living internationally. Some will be much to your liking; others not so much. But it all makes for a good story.

Returning to the theme of acquiring your home-country favorites, another way to be resupplied was to task your inbound colleagues with absolutely critical, but not liquid, items (as my brother found out, hauling Dr. Pepper over to Germany, due to my German brother having developed a strong attachment to it—half the cans exploded in his luggage during the flight). For us, this was often white cheddar cheese popcorn. Maybe because I had been an expat, I was particularly attuned to those requests. As the incoming globe-trotter, I would often bring a specific type of candy bar, or a gum, or an over-the-counter medicine not available locally that an overseas colleague asked me to pack-mule over. Even if you haven't been an expat, when traveling to meet an overseas-based colleague, at least ask if there is something small and simple you can bring. I have heard of companies allowing as a benefit one large box a year (say a good-sized packing box—not a sea container) of stuff. But I think that was to more remote locations than a major city.

Mailing things overseas is a whole other category of potential challenges for the expat on assignment. When in the Navy, they had a stateside PO box that would send all family and other mail along. Not exactly promptly but close enough. We did have an issue with a sheepskin rug purchased in Australia. It took more than four months to (apparently) travel from Australia to the US and back to our home in Japan. But it did make it. In Malaysia, we initially had to pay our own mail-forwarding service, as that was not an expat perk at the time. I can highly recommend the group Personal Mail International, Inc., based in New Jersey; they were outstanding. Once a week (or maybe twice a month? my memory fades), we would get all the mail that was not junk forwarded to the office in Kuala Lumpur. It wasn't cheap, per se, but it was very effective. Also, when the smog/smoke issue hit, we wondered (this is before the internet became all the shopping rage it currently is) how we would get some proper masks. One of the ladies in the mail-forwarding company had a weekend hobby of running a farm and knew exactly what to get. She bought the masks along with spare filters, added the cost to our monthly bill, and sent along the gear. Eventually, company policy changed, and now the company became the clearinghouse, which saved us a bit of money. That was just as I was starting my masters degree; hence all those Amazon book orders went domestic to the company mailroom and once a week over by courier to me. Also, the company librarians were wonderful. If there was a paper or book in the company's library, they would loan it to me via the weekly courier delivery just as if I had walked in the door to check it out.

Back to not so great, on my final international assignment, I was back to no mail-service reimbursement. In this case, we elected to not bother, as we had almost eliminated using snail mail anyway. It was also now deep into the internet age, and scans and attachments were commonplace. Some countries do not have the house-to-house postal system that the US does. If you wish, you may rent a post box, but delivery to a home or apartment only occurs by courier. Otherwise, you end up with an address akin to "Hotel Perfection, corner of Maple and Duvall Streets" or "Acme Business, Inc., Highway 5, across from the PepsiCo Bottling Plant." In this case, we were living in a serviced apartment associated with a large hotel, so we tried that hotel's address.

That doesn't work so well for your new credit card or ATM card. I needed my new ones and had to have them sent. We had tried the real mail system with something innocuous, and that made it. But when we then had the bank send the cards that way, they never appeared. We had to cancel the cards in absentia, reorder, and send by courier. In my first expat assignment, we had lived by having money wired monthly from our US bank to our Malaysian bank. That usually worked out fine (there was, of course, an unreimbursed wire fee, part of the cost of getting the wonderful experience of the assignment). I note "usually," as there were a few tense times when something wasn't quite right. On my stateside business trips, I made sure to bring the banking ladies a few nice trinkets from Malaysia as thanks.

In the Middle East, I lived off of credit cards and an ATM card. So, when I needed the new ATM card, this caused a panic. I had to quickly open a local bank account so I could wire myself some money. I started with visits to the usual international banks, but they wanted ludicrous amounts of money to open an account—up to $100,000 in one case. I finally came across a local bank that was satisfied with a small amount—more like a hundred bucks. And they threw in a local credit card (which was useful, as sometimes that credit card verification link via the internet back to the US just didn't work, and I had to use the local card). I had a wonderful experience with this bank for my remaining five-plus years in the region. In fact, they were so effective and customer friendly I tried to use them when I opened the new branch office in Abu Dhabi (turns out we had a deal with another major international bank, and I was not allowed to go local—that story later in the book). If you end up in Abu Dhabi, do look up Abu Dhabi Commercial Bank as a local banking option. (That is *not* a paid advertisement—just giving credit where credit is due.)

There is also the topic of taxation. Yes, there is a generous exemption the IRS allows for expatriate income. But the days of 100 percent are long, long gone—disappeared in the 1970s. Now there is a cap with inflationary growth. To put it in rough perspective, since all your kids' schooling, the home vacation trip benefit, and the (probably) higher housing and car rental costs are counted as income, all those will frequently eat away at that entire exemption. A single person or a couple that has no school-age kids may still reap a modest benefit, but the emphasis is on the word modest. I cannot count the different ways companies go about calculating the tax benefit. Some are straight off the top; others are tax equivalency, meaning they pay the tax, but siphon some amount back off your salary using a formula they consider fair (which means "you won't like it," I am sure). Some let you fend for yourself and provide a stipend and recommended accounting house to help. It is frankly arcane to me how they pick policy. But I did learn a lot about the options via research into the IRS website directly (which I can highly recommend—yes, I know—you are booing me now, but after NOAA's weather website, it is one I most frequently visit), as it did allow me enough information to logically refute a new expatriate taxation policy. In the end, we were forced to try it two ways—one with the company doing everything, and one where we did it ourselves. For the former, it was complicated by having kids and a comprehensive package; the latter was just us, and we did it with TurboTax. But there are good websites out there. We also contacted a very knowledgeable tax service who definitely had the right attitude on expatriate taxes—Taxes for Expats. She also has an affordable consultation option to help you research your tax situation before committing.

The final word on expatriate packages is ... they are all different. This causes a problem if it is different internal to a company (not associated with rank or job description). But outside, compare all you want. You will anyway, but every time I did, I found some things I liked about the other guy's package and some I didn't. On my final expat assignment, for instance, one of my friends already in-country with another company chatted with me on the topic. He thought my car allowance was pitiful but whistled with envy at my housing allowance. Therefore, I would tell my folks working for me to not get too enamored of someone else's package without *all* the details. As for comparing internally, I think that should be one of the supervisor's top human resources tasks: keep the packages fair. It can be a hard thing to accomplish, especially from ten thousand miles away.

For an American family locating overseas, Malaysia ended up being an ideal place for a first expatriate assignment. Sixty percent Malay-Muslim, 30 percent Chinese, and 10 percent Indian gave us a wonderful exposure to all three of these cultures that were somewhat lacking in St. Louis, Missouri (at least in the 1990s). As the Malaysian tourism quip went, "All of Asia is in Malaysia!" It was a great cultural experience for the entire family.

NightPigs and Other Mares

There I was ... family on vacation at one of the most important national parks in the country. It was literally in the middle of nowhere. The end of the earth was not quite visible due to the huge trees in the way, but it was there.

We had a great time getting to the park up a river in very uncomfortable, narrow, rickety, two- and three-person boats. While there, we filled the days and nights with local tours by guides who were excellent. A few incidents stood out.

First, we ate every day at the resort restaurant, which was open air. It was a logical choice for a usually hot and humid environment. However, it did have its peculiarities. The first were a couple of hornbill birds (large birds with huge bills) who had learned that these upright, hairless, walking bipeds had food. We at least only tossed them fruit (their normal food), but to have a three-foot bird honking at your table while you try to eat is, well, unique (their long beaks were not hard like a parrot's, so feeding them was easy—but best if you just lightly tossed that melon for them to catch).

Then there was the monkey buffet. We were sitting, mostly postdinner (and after feeding the hornbills) when I noticed a smallish monkey on the dessert section of the buffet—gobbling as much food as he could! As I watched, the kitchen door opened, and the little simian swept all the desserts off into his belly and jumped for the porch rail, the cook staff none the wiser.

We were headed back to our cottage for the night when my daughter came running back after running forward. Something ominous was going on! Turns out wild boars were rooting around (we are talking hundreds of pounds of walking bacon here), and she had accidentally startled them. Several nights, we heard them sharpening their tusks on the pilings holding up the cottage.

And, of course, a bat cave tour with—guess what: bat guano. My wife chose to *not* enter the bat cave. But the other three of us (my two preteen kids and I) followed our guide in. It was a remarkable experience. As soon as we disturbed the bats, they all fluttered within inches of our faces in the relative dark. The guide was only disappointed that none of the bat-eating snakes were on hand to make a snap. After sliding through a lot of guano getting out, my wife banished all of us to the back of the boat, made us strip at the cottage door, and thank heavens for resort laundry, or all the clothes would have been pitched.

Moral: Your wife may not have a sense of humor about bat guano, so carefully plan your tours.

Every culture is a bit different, but in Malaysia you have the wonderful blend of Malay, Chinese, and Indian with associated Muslim, Buddhist, and Hindu religions. In Malaysia, they celebrated everybody's holy days. And since all three never overlapped permanently, you could always go shopping. I had all three ethnic groups on my staff at one point or another. Every culture has its quirks, and one of the challenges (and fun part, for me) was learning how to navigate all the different cultures. For instance, when I went to move the office the first time, I was offered a steal of a deal on an already outfitted office right across the street from where we were and right next door to the hotel my business colleagues usually chose. But this got nixed in a heartbeat. It was on the fourth floor, and the number four is considered very unlucky in Chinese, as it sounds like the word for death. Not even my non-Chinese staff (Indian and Malay) would support the move. I once got a family vacation airline quote from my local travel agency that was for 14,444 ringgit (the local Malaysian currency). I asked her, laughing, if she would seriously issue me a plane ticket whose price had four fours! Got a laugh but also a blush, and when we finally picked the final route, there wasn't a four in the number.

The tour was also generally rewarding for me professionally. As the in-country program director, I had to do a little bit of everything: exports and ITAR; offset negotiations and support; logistics; operational planning; business and diplomatic meetings; and golf. Yes, on my first trip (to include house hunting as well as meeting my future customers), I was pretty much asked only two questions: (1) What was my golf handicap? (I said, "My swing.") (2) What kind of Harley Davidson did I own? Now I was too old to learn how to fall off a Harley, so I started for the first time in my life to make a serious effort at golfing. I was replacing someone who had a low single-digit golf handicap. I was with him once when he shot a seven over par while barefoot with beat-up rental clubs on a course he had never played. For the record, I failed miserably in this task. While I was a good companion and host and gave my partners lots to chuckle about, I don't think I ever got to an honest twenty-four handicap in spite of a company-paid club membership for six years.

On the business side, there were also cultural lessons to be learned. No bone-crushing handshakes, to start with. A polite, almost sliding shake was the local custom, usually with your left hand placed against your chest and a hint of a bow. Schedule was a peculiar concept. The entire region, with perhaps the exception of Singapore, is not a place for someone who is tied to a precision watch. On one meeting, I admittedly arrived a bit early to an unfamiliar location to make sure I was on time. The next couple of gents didn't show until a bit after time, making me nervous I was at the correct complex. We all went up to the office, turned on the air-conditioning, and started some coffee. As we sat politely chatting, the final (and highest ranking) gent called me to offer his apologies and say he was running late. Nonplussed, I said not to worry, I was also running late and still driving to the location but almost there. After I hung up, I saw the other two gents smiling very broadly. One of them said, roughly, "That was great! Very sensitive to our local culture!" I never heard if they told their colleague the real story or not. Other cultural differences were every bit as pronounced but also a bit harder for an American to adjust to in certain situations. Gender roles were definitely different. I had the luxury of bringing my wife more roses in five years than she would get the entire rest of her life—both before and after. They were cheap (except for the week around Valentine's Day), and the local flower shop lady came to know and expect me. I would get a dozen roses for two to three US dollars. One time I got eighteen for two bucks, as it was closing time, and she gave me what she had. But one day, while I was waiting as she trimmed and wrapped them, she was railing to a friend in the store in Malay. I could just barely get the drift that her husband was in the doghouse for something. As she handed the roses to me, she did manage a smile and say, "Men—aarrgh!" This was definitely not the US.

Battle of the Sexes

There I was ... learning a lesson in cultural (in)sensitivity. I was asked to support a meeting for planning an upcoming airshow. My company was a big supporter, and the organizer thought I would be an asset working with the local ministry of defense. I met the organizer's people at the MOD main gate—two very cute young ladies. We headed in to talk to the assistant undersecretary of something—that is, an old guy. We got the usual coffee and tea and moved on to business ... kind of. This guy spent much of the meeting telling these gals how cute they were and touching a knee or elbow. They spent the meeting giggling and attempting to keep the discussion on target. I did my part offering company support and support of the US embassy (which I knew would be forthcoming). As we were leaving, the undersecretary suggested they meet again later in the week for lunch (but not with me).

We collected our identification and left the premises. At that point, comfortably out of earshot, I turned to the ladies and expressed my horror, as an American, at what they had just gone through in terms of harassment and apologized for a male colleague's behavior. To my amazement, they just laughed. They said it happens all the time here, and they were used to it, and nothing ever comes of it. I said it wouldn't happen now in the US. Of course, this was a country that still ran hiring advertisements requesting good "front-office appearance" and that resumes should have a photo—long after the US had abandoned that bit.

I did have a receptionist—nice young Indian gal—who was talking about the possibility that the US president would be in town (he ended up sending the VP). I said I wasn't going to let her around him, given his reputation with women. She giggled and said, "I wouldn't mind." Eesh. One of my older colleagues in town on a business trip was flirting with her as he left the office; this guy was quite fun but obviously considered himself a bit of a ladies' man. He left her giggling as he returned to the hotel. Her comment: "That Joe—such a character. I wish he were my uncle." I left the office laughing on that note. I had the delight in telling Joe later that night her comment, and he was devastated. He had hoped to be considered for a younger role.

Moral: Gender equality is another culture-specific situation. When confronted with a disparity between your culture and your client's culture, you must be adaptable. Polite but adaptable.

I, of course, took to attempting to learn Malay as I was living there. This was not to the liking of my staff, as the previous guy and my other office mate made little attempt at the language. But as I progressed, the staff started to stop talking among themselves. I was never great, but I was politely conversant and could discuss my family and help a taxi driver get around. On a trip to one ministry, I was waiting politely at the main desk of the open-seating secretarial pool while the head secretary went off to get some document. One of the nice young ladies, without obviously looking up, said to her friends in Malay, "Oh, he's cute!" I then said in my best Malay, "Thank you! So are you!" And the place started to crack up. Out came the head secretary, having heard the exchange, who asked in Malay if I was married. I said, in Malay, "Oh yes—wife and two children." Her reply, with a huge grin, was, "Oh, too bad!" By now, the poor young lady who had started the conversation looked like she wanted to crawl under her desk. When I went back for my doctoral research some twelve years after leaving the country, I still recalled enough Malay to get a driver with no real English capability to all the locations I needed to get. Anyway, back to the culture. Balancing the needs of a program and the local culture was some of the most diplomatically sensitive work I have ever done. And it wasn't necessarily all on the customer's end. I had to work with my own folks to keep them on the straight and narrow.

How Not to Build Infrastructure

There I was … reviewing on a weekly basis the base upgrade for the new aircraft. I went up once a week for three years.

I commiserated with the one lonely field rep there for two years, then with the twenty folks we had on base for the next year, and finally the eight or so remain-behind field technicians who were still there after I left three years later. I watched all the buildings get built or modified. For the first few months, I went up and back in a single but long day. For the rest, I remained overnight and made two trips to the base. I was on first-name basis with the singers and hostesses in the nice downtown hotel. It made it easy to arrive and depart, as—while a poor security measure—I did exactly the same thing every trip.

Back to building a base. New buildings were being raised. I had to gently cajole the public works department to make the buildings sound for our support equipment. I eventually got along quite well with the national head of public works; we had frequent meetings in both the capital and at the base. He became very open. When I complained one day about the lack of progress on the electrical systems, his reply was, "What do you expect? The contractor ran off with the money!" I asked why there was no immediately planned prosecution. "Politically connected award" was the reply. A shame.

One of the buildings going up was a pilot flight simulator; the building was public work's responsibility, but the installation of the simulator itself was our responsibility. The technical lead was a subcontractor whose man on site was a hotheaded Italian American. I would visit him each week, and he would give me an earful about how the locals weren't doing things correctly. As an example, the holding structure, instead of being of easily modifiable wood or steel, was of concrete. When it ended up an inch too high and an inch too wide, they had to hand-chip everything out. This was driving my subcontract lead crazy.

We had a program management review one week. All the local bigwigs came in. I was present for the major confrontation. The building was not being completed in time and was holding up the progress on the simulator. One of the locals at the end of a long exchange said, "Well, as God wills," which led to the ill-thought-out snapped reply from my subcontract lead, "God has nothing to do with this incompetence!" That statement led to my forceful intervention. I grabbed this guy and hauled him around the corner of a building and said that was totally inappropriate. He just sneered. I then went back and apologized for my subcontractor's cultural insensitively. The reply by the locals, "He is entirely correct but is also entirely incorrectly presenting his case." I had to call my boss that night—never a good situation. I only called him when I had a crisis, and the secretary's voice on hearing mine was a reflection of that. She said, "I'll track him down in a moment. Just hang on." Note to self: call the boss with good news occasionally.

The next day, still at the site review, the subcontractor lead came up and asked me for a word in private. I thought I was going to get both barrels, but instead I got a very contrite message. "I have received and understood your message. I now know if you call your boss again, I'm fired. So, I'm all in on fixing this as culturally sensitively as can be done." I reminded him he could unload on me as much as he wanted but to hold off on the locals and let me do that; that was my job, not his. He finished the job in spectacular fashion.

Morals: International business may not be for everyone. Not all overseas businesses move at the same pace as US business. I have seen faster paces as well as slower. But as the outlier representing both your company and, indirectly, your country, you cannot lose your cool. And the international manager is often that solo outlier that the locals deal with.

One of the skills I have acquired over the years is that of bridging cultural communication gaps. This is extremely vital to long-term program success. The first step is to listen very carefully. Read a good book on listening skills. For Americans especially, we seem to always be in transmit mode. The Finns were very good at this. They would sit quietly and let the American or Americans drone on and on about something, spilling the beans in the process on one issue or another. But as much as they came to like and respect me, I was frustrating for them. I kept my answers short and direct and would just stop and outwait them in the silence game. As far as I could tell, I was the only one to do so. I would also frequently listen to both sides of a discussion and realize each side of the table was talking past the other. I would insert a small clarification, or I would rephrase a question, and suddenly it would click, and the answer would be clear.

Send the Real Engineers

There I was ... back at the base with my field engineers checking on the real end user.

In this case, I was helping inspect the new logistics warehouse. I was walking with a US government facilities engineer who was in town checking out the installations. We kept finding sinks near a door that had a shower behind it. Curiosity finally overcame our cultural inhibitions, and we politely asked what they were for. "Those are the emergency wash and showers stations as specified for this facility." Oh boy. On the drive back to the hotel, the engineer said he thought he had something that could work to explain the situation. The next day, he arrived with pages torn out of a product catalog (who but an engineer carries a technical product catalog?) that showed current US emergency eye wash and emergency shower wash down station products.

The local engineers took one look—I swear less than ten seconds—and instantly knew what should have been done. We didn't make a big deal of it, but a month later all the sinks and showers were out, and proper emergency eye wash and wash down stations were installed. The bosses had made the good-deal trip to the US installations but had not taken any engineers or any operable notes.

Moral: Send the real engineers when you are having to design a new facility, and as the international manager, be aware when setting up your program. If it includes technology transfers and over-the-shoulder training, you need to insist on qualified (or qualifiable) personnel from your local partners—industry or government.

One of the simplest, almost funny, examples was in the middle of negotiating a framework contract. The Malaysian government wanted the costs of bank wires to be paid by the contractor. As it was done via a Malaysian bank, we wanted them to cover the cost, since, theoretically, we could not control what would be charged. I think we spent an hour discussing just this point. I finally asked the group, to no one in particular, what cost level are we talking about? No one knew. We took a break while one of the Malaysians ran to the office to make a call. On returning, the Malaysian said, rather sheepishly, fifty Malaysian ringgit, or about fifteen US dollars. After a moment of silence, my boss said, "We'll cover the cost." Yet we spent an hour in a room with fifteen people arguing about it until the proper question was asked. But there were much more delicate situations that had to be addressed.

How to Fire a Local

There I was … helping my lone logistics guy bring in forty-foot sea containers full of parts. We were attempting to bring in a lot of spare parts and have them properly stored in a local warehouse. This was new logistical technology for the local military, and we were getting some reasonable offset credit for it.

Enter my solo, mainly-on-his-own field rep. I would go up weekly to check his morale. He was initially very jaded, as my predecessor had rarely come up. But as I went week on week, he finally warmed up and began to share his true concern: parts were coming in faster than his twelve-person local team could process. He attributed part of this to their leadership. He asked for help. That's my job. I went into the military headquarters and met with the colonel in charge of the program's logistics. We had a polite conversation that revolved obliquely around the leadership of the logistics parts induction program. After a coffee and tea or two, he asked me to wait while he dialed. We then went up to the general in charge of all air force logistics. Another round of coffee. In the end, the two gents were discussing the officer in question—wrong man for the job, but what could they do? They could transfer him elsewhere—I think a military course. And then not refill the position for a bit. "But you didn't hear any of this, correct?" "Not a word," was my reply. Sure enough, three weeks later, the officer was transferred. Things started to improve immediately.

Moral: International business involves a very intricate and delicate interaction between multiple parties—the provider (your company), the recipient local entity, and the two interlocutors: you, the business-development manager, and your counterpart in the government office. You have to delicately handle many situations, most of them driven by personalities. Enjoy your job!

The more dissimilar your culture is from theirs, the more challenging and rewarding is the cross-cultural interaction. It was during my time in Malaysia that I had one of the most rewarding periods in my academic life. I was invited to join a master's program with a focus on international security studies and diplomacy. Managed by the National University of Malaysia but sponsored by the Ministry of Foreign Affairs, the class consisted of about twenty Malaysians—mainly government servants and military officers, all on a one-year sabbatical. There were five of us not from Malaysia: Japan, Vietnam, Mauritius, Sierra Leone, and me. Yes, not only was I the only Western extraction person in the class, I was one of only two of us who had to still work full-time at the job. I'd be up early to clear emails at the office, head into class for about six hours, then return to the office to clear messages and emails before heading home to study. If I had an important meeting request, or when the boss came to town, then I had to skip class for a day or a week. All this with two kids in grade school. By this point in my job, I had moved from program management to business development, so I did not travel as frequently to the base where our field representatives were. But travel some I still did (not to mention the unexpected death of my father, necessitating a short, tiring family flight home for the funeral).

Death. There is no real way to disguise the issue. People die while on overseas assignments. I was fortunately spared the issue during my time abroad, but one of my colleagues had to handle it from the US. The gent in question had passed away in a chair in his hotel room in Thailand. Pity the hotel staff that has to, after a couple of days, force open a locked door and be faced with this situation. That is one reason many hotels now have a Do Not Disturb limit of a couple of days; they need to know you are still alive. The guy in question had had a heart attack sitting in a chair watching TV. The US embassy was fully on board with the repatriation of remains—good to note. But my buddy was still down one internationally experienced logistician. These are also issues that pervade international business. Most folks do not intend to die overseas, but some do.

But back to international studies, my overall course was extremely satisfying. You do not normally get to take such a course with many diverse (read antipathetic) opinions of your own worldview. Malaysia was exceptional in its mix of Malay, Indian, and Chinese cultures. They all had an impact on the local Malaysian culture. This was perhaps best typified by the local cuisine—a mix of all three. As the Malaysian tour bus guide told us in the first week, "We hate each other's guts, but we love each other's food!"

Yellow Lantern

There I was ... a dare by Eddie, my local ethnic Chinese driver in Penang.

Really? Yes, we had driven by this Thai restaurant a dozen plus times, and each time he said, "You cannot take the spice!" I, as a proud Texan of course, always said, "Oh contraire," but it was not until one of my later trips to Penang—when I was going up for an overnighter regularly—that I made the challenge solid: I'd buy, we'd eat.

Boy, was that *hot*! He had arranged for a table in the back, by the kitchen. I let him order, and we shared. He had nibbles to cool the heat; I had a weak beer. After the first five bites, we were both sweating. Yes, Thai can be excruciatingly hot. But you cannot give up the test! I think I sweated through two shirts that evening. Eddie also was sweating, but now we were in the mano a mano phase—death before dishonor! We ate to our heart's content. Then I paid the bill and headed to the hotel.

A side story with the same gent comes to mind when I had my boss and a couple of colleagues in tow. I was getting ribbed by him and the others in the car—surely, I knew the seedier side of Penang. I didn't, and don't call me Shirley. But I went ahead and called their bluff. I asked Eddie, "Where are the women?" Nonplussed, he asked, "Quick and easy or hard and complicated?" Ha! My compatriots ultimately did not want either, and I could watch Eddie smirk.

Moral: Don't eat Thai unless you have the gut for it.

Continuing my international master's theme, at first, I was looked on with great suspicion by most of the class. I even had one of my thesis advisors ask me in private if I really worked for the CIA. But this course of study was squarely in my interest areas. I had kept that promise to myself never to take another class again that I didn't want to learn about. The course was almost like falling out of bed. I could almost write a paper then just go find the footnotes. My popularity increased when, early on, I started sharing my books. As the "rich American," I bought all the recommended titles and then some. Since the company graciously sent all my Amazon book orders over to me in a weekly shipment, I could order US domestic and within a few days have the readings. I'd hand the books off to my fellow students, who would then go copy the desired reading for everyone. In the end, I had more books than I needed to keep, and after first letting my classmates dig through the pile for books they particularly liked, I donated the rest to the school's library.

Two-Shift Motivation

There I was … another routine base visit and checkup on my Lone Ranger helping the locals manage the inflow of thousands of spare parts.

After the obstructionist leader was moved, my field engineer on site still faced how to handle the incoming spares. After a couple of weeks of slow progress, on my next trip I saw all smiles.

"What's up?" "We are gaining at an incredible rate!" Whoa! Great news. I asked how that had happened. The reply was that the junior officer, now temporarily in charge, had instituted a radical reorganization (at least for the local staff): a two-shift workweek. I was most complimentary to my guy and his local counterpart.

At the bar later, I learned from my guy, now in private, the definition of two-shift. Half the staff worked for twelve hours on one day, then had an entire day off; the other half then worked the next twelve-hour day. So, both groups got every other day off. In that fashion, they cleared several months' backlog in a few weeks. As soon as they went back to regular shifts (i.e., all twelve of them for eight hours a day), the backlog began to grow. Every third or fourth month, they'd go on two-shift for a bit and clear it. Amazing what motivates!

Moral: Same with international business, it is amazing what motivates. That is the crux of an international business manager's job: find that motivator and use it.

Returning to my second master's, the students, as they warmed to me, began to include not just me but my entire family in Hindu Deepavali, Chinese New Year, and Muslim Hari Raya celebrations. It was wonderful to learn all these holidays that, before living in Malaysia, I really didn't know existed. I also got to participate in many lecture series. These were a little bit of a pain—often evening events—but I did get to hear Fidel Castro speak at one, and only for an hour or so (he apparently was a famously long-winded speaker). We also took a class field trip to the Philippines and China, where we had interactions with academicians and policy writers.

The Only White Guy

There I was ... literally the only Caucasian in a sea of Chinese students and parents. I was on my master's class trip to Beijing, and we had two days of touring built in. I had already been to Beijing with my family and seen all the usual local tourist sites. The first tour day for my class was the Forbidden City and the Summer Palace. They are wonderful, but I didn't need a second visit. I did go back to the Great Wall with my classmates, as when I was there on family vacation, a sandstorm had rolled in, and we couldn't get the real grandeur. But on the first tour day with my classmates, I excused myself and went instead to visit the Chinese museum of military history.

China has been at war in one way or another for at least four thousand years. I don't need to remind my dear reader that one of the most famous tracts in military strategy is *The Art of War*, written by the Chinese master Sun Tzu sometime around 500 BCE. So, their military museum could cover a lot of topics. As I recall, it was five stories high in a huge building. Starting on the ground floor, you were taken through the entire history—in posted explanations in both Chinese and English. This only stopped when I finally got to the top floor and the Korean War; then it was only in Chinese. A bit unfair, as I would have loved to know their version of the events.

Anyway, during my three-plus-hour visit to the museum, I was the only western DNA in the place. I saw many of the kids looking at me, often wide-eyed. But everyone was very polite, all smiles when eye contact was made, no pointing, no obviously obnoxious comments. (This was unlike a passing sneer while with the German Navy in the UK twenty years prior. A couple of teenagers snarled something like "F———cking Nazis" as we passed on a street. I turned and snapped, "Who are you calling a Nazi?" in my clear American accent. Their astonished faces were priceless, and they almost walked into a light post looking backward at me and my friends.)

After the museum, I took my uniqueness to ... wait

for it ... McDonald's Golden Arches, just across the street! Thankfully, most restaurants in Asia use picture menus. You don't have to speak the language; you just point and smile. I was still the only white guy, and the kids were still staring at me but still in awe. Earlier in Beijing with my family, we had numerous local families, also on (domestic) vacations, come up to take pictures of their kids with our kids (then about ten and thirteen years old)—my daughter especially, who had very long, blond hair. We even had older ladies want pictures with her, and at least one made the sign of snipping a lock of her hair—apparently a good luck charm! (She didn't actually snip.)

Moral: Even if you are not destined to do business in a country, it is still worth a look around. You never know what stories you will come up with that will be useful as examples when you do get questioned on your interest in other cultures.

Back to the class trip. By this point, the class had informally designated me to be the "first-question person" after the talk or introductory remarks. On the conclusion, everyone would look at me and smile, and I had to come up with the first tough ... but not too tough ... question for the lecturer or panel. In China, the Chinese panel—mainly of retired officers of flag rank—had looked at me in almost stupefaction, as they had expected a bunch of Malaysians, and there was this white guy smiling at them. I began to earn my keep, so to speak, with my classmates on this trip. In this meeting, for example, I heard the following "joke" from one of the panelists. They likened Southeast Asia to a house with several rooms, most of them occupied by beautiful women. But in the middle was a large and powerful man. The comment was that the women should keep their doors securely locked to keep that man from entering in the middle of the night. My Malaysian colleagues were not at all pleased with the analogy. I think it was one of the few times my classmates welcomed the presence of an American in their master's class. With a snarl, I could put paid to those kinds of not-so-subtle threats. When I have been asked why countries should count on the US, I have often retorted, "So, name another country with a dozen aircraft carriers and a half dozen amphibious units ready to help you if invaded." The silence is deafening.

After their minilecture came my first question, which was, "Why don't you export more military equipment?" That brought an unexpected result. We were talking strictly through a translator, but before she could translate, one of the panel snorted and said quietly, "Because it is crap." The official response, translated both ways, was, of course, more politically correct. In the Philippines, one of our lecturers was a real conspiracy theorist and railed on US involvement in the region. I got to ask him if he was a die-hard Communist or only a sunny-day Communist, much to the chuckles of my classmates. The course overall was a great experience, and in the end, I had a couple of my essays as well as my thesis published by the university and a regional political science magazine.

Shopping internationally is almost a cliché of interesting objects de art and exotic foods to be tried or weapons to be bought and returned to your home. From the boomerangs of Australia (some beautifully crafted and made to workable by an amateur) to the elaborate Kris daggers of Malaysia and Indonesia with their fine metal work, it all makes for wonderful additions to your "I have been there" cabinet. But what about the more mundane stuff, especially when you are living overseas? This is where the fine art of expat networking or pass down from your predecessor comes in to play.

The fine art of negotiating can be a cultural phenomenon. In many cultures, you are expected to negotiate, and there is a little loss of face for the shopkeeper if you just paid asking. Even my wife learned in Malaysia, in the department store, to conclude the discussion with "Best price?" almost always got an extra 5 percent off (not on the groceries but on the clothes, furniture, etc.). But negotiation is not for everyone. For instance, my wife had to learn it gradually.

Asian Negotiation

There I was … in Hong Kong for the first time with my wife. It was almost like the honeymoon we really didn't get after the wedding. This was back in the mid-1980s, well before the UK handover back to the PRC had occurred in 1997. It was just a fun place to be for shopping, dining, and sightseeing—possibly part of that being the reunion with my wife after several months of separation while underway. Having returned since then a couple of times on transpacific flight stopovers, it was still a fun place to be—but just a bit more controlled feeling.

We were on a bus/harbor tour that included a stop at a night market. I reminded her we were supposed to be prepared to negotiate. As we wandered through the market, she stopped in front of a stand with silk pajamas. "How much?" The merchant mentioned a price. Before I could intervene, my wife immediately blurted out, "Wow! That is cheap!" I still remember the smirk on the merchant's face. Yep, we paid asking price.

We did better in Southeast Asia with some rosewood furniture, and by the time I was living in the Middle East (yet another decade later), she had the negotiation thing down pat.

Moral: Negotiate. Don't give it away. Silk PJs are chump change, but international programs are not. Never go in with your BAFO (that is, your best and final offer, which a giggling wife is not). Understand your spread well and the limits of your authority.

If you are going international, you should read a good book on negotiating. Creating a viable BAFO is a good case in point. Your dilemma is that you do not know what any competitors may be offering. You do not want to start too high and be disqualified early on before you even get to the BAFO phase. My favorite BAFO story came from colleagues working Korea extensively. On one major procurement, after months and months of negotiations, all three competitors were called into a room in the procurement agency and seated at different tables. In walked several of the senior procurement officers. They said briefly, "All three of your offers are technically and programmatically acceptable. We are, therefore, going to decide this program on cost." Each company was given a sheet of paper and a heavy envelope and told to write their BAFO down and seal it. Each envelope was picked up, and the committee retired to the adjacent room. They returned in a few minutes with three new envelopes and sheets of paper. "No one was low enough. Do it again." This process was repeated several times that afternoon, until the committee returned finally, with big similes, and said a winner had been selected. "Thank you all very much for a cooperative and comprehensive competition, and congratulations to the Acme Company!" I, too, had a very similar, if less dramatic, BAFO discussion. We had also been told our offer and the competition's were considered technically equal. We were given a day to return with a BAFO. My boss and I sat looking at each other for a couple of hours at the hotel bar that night, trying to read the minds of both the customer and the competition. We did make a cut in the cost and threw in some additional items free of charge. But it was not good enough; in the usual business phrase, the other company was hungrier. We just hoped we had driven the competition a lot lower than we would have previously. Because many cultures grow up negotiating, you are already starting from behind with your big-box-store mentality.

Another Asian Negotiation

There I was … amazingly, my second trip to Beijing in a year. This time I was in Beijing with my master's classmates.

One afternoon was devoted to shopping. I really

didn't have anything to buy, but one of my lady class-mates insisted I get something for the missus. So, after wandering a bit, I found some lingerie that might be fun. The lady had said to not make any sign, express any interest, and let her do the negotiation. I wandered out and around the corner and told her what I'd buy. "I'll take care of it." I watched her for probably fifteen minutes. She walked in, walked out, pointed, walked away at least twice, and finally returned with the negligee—at half what I would have paid. Payback was me adding two suitcases to my return flight, as I was business class and they would be included at no cost. Fun conclusion was on returning home, one of our classmates was on sabbatical from the customs office and knew all the folks at the airport. There was no duty-free limit for us that trip! Clink, clink, clink …

Moral: Remember both parties have to want the deal for it to be concluded. The other side is also obligated to negotiate as hard as they can. But a deal can generally be reached for a win-win situation.

Being on a long-term international assignment can be an excellent experience. One aspect is the ability to visit countries you would not nor-mally afford as a middle-class American. Our six family years overseas gave us opportunities for family vacations in China, Cambodia, Vietnam, Greece, Italy, Germany, France, Egypt, Israel, and Jordan just to click off a few. Our kids got quite the exposure; my wife remembers my daughter coming home from a sixth-grade class once back in the US permanently, saying approximately, "Wow, we were talking about Egypt today, and I have seen all the sights in person, and no one else has." In Cambodia, my daughter was annoyed because her brother, who was running a high fever with a flu, got to stay in the hotel all day playing on the computer, while we made her go for at least half of each day's tours with us. The Angkor Wat complex was magnificent. The tour of the capital, Phnom Penh, was sobering, with its collection of memorabilia for all those who died in their terrible civil war. But I do recall an impressive sight not on the tourist list. We were staying at the Raffles Hotel—wonderful. But late at night, across from the hotel, was a dimly lit edifice. I asked the concierge what it was, and he said, "Local college." As dark and dim as it was, hundreds of young adults were making their way there to improve their future prospects. Everywhere we went, folks in Cambodia were working hard. I even saw them making a paved asphalt road by hand: small rocks and tar, then larger rocks being smashed to smaller rocks. I asked if this was prison labor, and the reply was, "No, it is the dry season,

and these are farmers working for the government for a little extra pay."
You really don't realize how good you have it in the US until you travel to
some places overseas. Both our guides, by the way, had lost both their
parents and many friends to the genocide instigated by the Khmer Rouge.

Tunnels and Water Turbines

There I was … this time with my son on a father-son,
military-focus vacation to Vietnam. I wanted to visit
Dien Bien Phu, the Hanoi "Hilton," and the Cu Chi
Tunnels. My wife and daughter gave it a pass to have
private mother-daughter shopping time in Malaysia.

We didn't have all the time we would have wished,
but we still had two great tour guides. The tunnels were
certainly interesting. The local guide was able to dis-
appear in front of our eyes by carefully pulling down
the lid. They had widened some of the tunnels for the
American tourists, but they also still had original tunnels left. Pointing to my son, the local guide indicated
that he thought my son would fit through. So, off they
went! Gone for about five minutes down one hole (which
I would not have fit in) and up another. Great time.

But one of the most interesting parts was our return
drive from Dien Bien Phu to Hanoi. We had not wanted
to waste a day so accepted what was a thirteen-hour
return drive. This certainly busted a number of my per-
ceptions of Vietnam. First, the country is packed with
people. My son and I had already taken half an hour at
the hotel in Hanoi to watch the mass of humanity ebb
and flow on bicycles and small motorcycles around the
front of the hotel, including two gents carrying between
them a twenty-foot ladder—by two motorcycles—one in
front and one behind.

Back to the return drive. Farms everywhere.
Farmers on the road going to the local market. At our
lunch stop, our guide went to buy some roasted chest-
nuts or something from an old man on the street. The
cost was a pittance, and the guide was going to buy everything. But the man didn't want to sell. He apparently
said, "If I sell you all of them, I won't have anything to
do for the rest of the day!" Also, along the way, I saw
hundreds—maybe thousands—of small wires running
to the river nearby the road. I asked what they were
for. They were attached to twelve-volt generators being
powered by the flow of the water. All the small huts

we passed had a small amount of electricity running to them—for cell phones, small TVs, and small lights. These guys were seriously trying to better themselves.

Final note: The Hanoi prison, while containing a small display on the US/Vietnam War, was mainly about the French/Vietnam resistance fight and the associated Vietnamese Resistance heroes. The guide was a bit nervous we would, as Americans, take offense. But none taken.

Moral: Helping countries' populations improve themselves works better when the populace is involved and dedicated. I do not believe I have ever seen as hardworking a population as I did in Vietnam and Cambodia.

Being an expatriate or even an internationalist does have its trying moments. Often the folks back at the headquarters think you are goofing off or having a super easy time. Your flights overseas they consider a perk, not a dreaded event fraught with delays, crappy food, cramped conditions, and crowds. Of course, they are not the ones up at midnight for that vital conference call, nor are they going in alone into various companies and ministries, trying to nudge progress on your programs or next sales. And when they do drop in for a visit, if you take care of them properly, well, he or she won't know how tough it really is to get all the dominoes lined up for a single push.

Boss at the Pool

There I was … having a major program review at the local air base. It was big enough that my boss's boss had flown in for the event. With so much being planned, I had arranged lots of different transportation. All us working stiffs went out early in the morning to make sure the base and setup was correct. This included my boss. Several hours later, the big boss was picked up in a limo and taken to the base—just in time to speak to and listen to a few appropriate remarks by senior customers and host a lunch for the soon-to-be minted squadron. After that, we sent him back to the hotel, partly so he could do email but mainly to get him out of our hair while the rest of us did some real work.

We dragged our tired and hot bodies back into the hotel right at sunset—a fifteen-hour day including get-up, travel, and work. The big boss hailed us from the swim-up pool bar with an umbrella drink in his hand.

He said, "Ya know, Mullet, this is an easy gig you have over here!" Easy for him.

Same big boss, by the way, who was crossing the street in the capital. The favored hotel was literally across six lanes of traffic from the office, but usually those six lanes were at a standstill in terms of traffic. He (and others) got into the practice of just wandering between the stopped cars from the hotel to the office building. Enter the local practice of small motorcycle (moped) drivers running between the cars. You had to always be on the lookout for them. One morning, out he walks to cross the street. Cars are at a dead stop, but he forgets to look for the mopeds and steps in front of one. This causes the driver to hit him at a nonfatal but reasonable speed, knocking him onto a car trunk. The moped goes careening like a pachinko ball, hitting another four or five cars. Of course, the driver immediately pops off the ground to scream at the big boss. But five car doors open as drivers go to scream at the moped driver, not having seen my big boss as the ultimate cause. Big boss quickly grabs his briefcase and dashes into the office building! At least for us, no harm, no foul, only a slightly bruised (and embarrassed) big boss.

Moral: Most of your company is going to think that you, the globe-trotting business-development manager racking up the frequent-flier miles, are getting a great deal! Not much you can do about it, except laugh (in private) when they get clocked by a moped.

Another aspect of international living is being where the action is. This may or may not be comfortable—my trips in the Middle East being a case in point. I was always a bit nervous flying into Beirut but, for some reason, not into most of the other countries in the region. I remember getting three calls on a single night in Malaysia. The first was from my mother (in the US) who said she had just seen the news about riots in the capital and asked if I was okay. Answer, "Yes." Then two of my closer field engineers from Penang called for the same question, and I gave the same answer. Now, family secret here, we had virtually stopped watching television and had no clue what was going on if it was not on the internet. But prompted by three phone calls, I did another NAFOD (no apparent fear of death) thing. I got into my car and drove right downtown, looking for the riots. Very disappointing—nothing to be seen. I later asked my embassy contacts what they had seen—also nothing. I think the one response was, "A single burning tire surrounded by maybe five people." While bad things can come up, the major news media often inflate it to make it sound impressive. On some days, I can wish I had experienced the drama seen in those little news clips. Turns out the big riot was a bunch of rambunctious petty thieves who took the opportunity of a nonviolent protest to steal a bunch of T-shirts—hardly a revolutionary moment.

Diving in Malaysia

There I was … wet again. I am not a huge diver, and I have now not worn tanks for so long I would get a refresher before plunging in. But I did a bit of diving in and around Malaysia. Its peninsular east coast and the coast off Sabah are world-class diving opportunities.

This time was a bit different. I got a call from my employee pilot still serving as the safety officer in the local squadron. He was asking if I would be willing to host a dinner. I often hosted dinners—usually quarterly or semiannually—when the squadron was on a detachment, usually with a golf game attached. This time the terms were different. The squadron was on an annual or biennial survival camp on the east coast. In exchange for supporting both the general squadron dinner and the officers' mess dinner, I'd get to scuba dive off a resort. *Resort* didn't sound too *survival* to me.

Background: My pilot was also a qualified scuba instructor. He had gradually qualified all the pilots in the squadron. To scuba, the squadron had purchased two boats for search and rescue. These were trailered over to the opposite coast and used to run out the squadron and all the gear for a week on a version of a desert island. Except where the officers were staying was actually a beachfront resort.

I got to the location via a convoluted process. Commercial flight up to the town near the base. C-130 transport to a remote and little-used airstrip. Helicopter (full of chairs for the dinner) out to the island. Sure enough, we had two days of great diving in clear, warm, tropical waters. I expensed (with my boss's permission) a general squadron barbeque and an officers' mess night complete with karaoke. My hut was nicely air-conditioned. I returned via the same torturous route.

Moral: In spite of all the work and travel, there will be moments like this that really make being international a unique experience. Enjoy!

Ah, yes, with the right connections, international business does have its perks. Just don't tell anyone back home, as they will then think they were correct in thinking your job is cushy.

Nine-eleven did give us some pause for thought. My mother called from the US and said dryly, knowing my habits, "Turn on your TV *now*." We saw the second plane hit the tower. I had my boss call within minutes and suggest strongly that I did not go into the office the next morning. I called my staff to let them know—knowing I did not watch TV, they were relieved that I knew—day off, planning later. I agreed to meet the other US member of my staff at an obscure coffee shop. I had it better than most Americans during that time. I was surrounded by horrified foreigners who called, texted, and emailed their contempt of the event. Every race, every religion was included. The average American did not get that instantaneous support, but I did. I knew the world was on our side within twenty-four hours. One vignette—apparently a couple of kids on a moped (small motorcycle) went driving by the US embassy showing an obscene hand gesture and were summarily flattened and arrested by the local police. There was no other show of support for the terrorists at all, and complete support for the US in its time of mourning. I had already been contacted to speak at an event organized by the Asia Pacific Center for Security Studies. The organization, sponsored by the US government, attempted to create an inclusive network throughout the Asia-Pacific region. I was invited as an expert in international industry. But, of course, I was arriving just five weeks after 9/11. Almost no one was going to Hawaii. My taxi ride to the hotel was sobering. "Bankrupt" was the statement from the driver. All tourists had cancelled. The hotel itself, lucky to be hosting the APCSS conference, had almost no one else. Tourism was off well over 80 percent of year-on-year levels. Restaurants were empty. The conference itself was good but somber. With more than three dozen nations represented, there was not a hint of a smirk in the group as they digested the terrible impact the attack on the US had caused—and this from some countries that would usually deride the US for its cultural hegemony. On leaving for the US, I was advised by the hotel to go to the airport four hours early. A credit to the newly formed TSA, I got through security within minutes and had three-plus hours to kill. This was repeated in every airport on my trip that fall; the universal recommendation was to go to the airport early, and each time I found massively improved security screening times. I was incredibly lucky, as TSA was working hard to reduce timelines, improve security, and get the nation back on its traveling feet.

Speaking of improving your travel experiences, here are a couple of notes from general experience. Global Entry is a program the Customs and Border Patrol (CBP) offers US citizens to expedite return entry to the US. It costs a bit, and you have to go for a screening appointment, but it is well worth the effort if you are a frequent international traveler. You get to skip the lines at immigration, either in the US or overseas (CBP now has many overseas "clear before you take off" locations, which is also nice). There are also programs for non-US citizens, but regrettably (if understandably) I don't have their exact information. If you are coming to the US a lot and not violating general US visa requirements (see later in the book), they are also worth it. I have seen long, long lines at immigration just due to the volume of people coming. It wasn't as if CBP had only one desk open; they had a dozen. Another thought—airline club lounge membership. It sounds snooty, but most lounges get you out of the hubbub of the general noise in the airport, get you free internet access and a place to plug your computer and phones, as well as a chance to drink and eat without paying a small fortune at the airport eateries. Internationally, if you are business class, you often get the lounge as a perk from your ticket. But if not, after that sixteen-hour coach flight to a three-hour layover, it is nice to get to a club for a shower and change. I do recall Osaka, Japan. It had a pay-as-you-go shower service—for about a dollar. Unique in my experience and well worth it. Even though I usually had lounge access, I would pay that buck to refresh myself before the next leg of the journey.

A final regional story to show how varied and intermingled the local cultures can be. When my wife and I had been in Thailand over a decade prior, we attended one of the almost-mandatory cross-dress evening entertainment acts. It was a fabulous musical, if a little loud. But now a decade on, in another location, I got to actually host a similar event.

Paper Dolls

There I was … getting ready for another party. This time, I was at least in near total control, as it was a local party. We were celebrating the launch of the squadron we had just helped establish. The celebration would include an extensive lunch for the enlisted personnel and a golf tournament and dinner with entertainment for the officers.

I was approached at a reasonable stage in the planning about the entertainment for the dinner event. The planning committee was just a couple of guys keeping everything under wraps. They asked what I would afford, and I said to give me some options. First option would have been great, a locally renowned singer, but her budget was out of my reach. However, the other offer was, after coordination, affordable. I gave them the go-ahead to book the act: the Paper Dolls.

You can probably guess the outcome, but here it is anyway. After an as-usual hot and humid golf tourney where I got nothing but a consolation prize, we headed for a nice local hotel. I cleaned up and went down to ensure organization was proceeding properly, as I had my boss and his boss (again) attending as guests of honor, along with all the officers of the squadron and all the supporting staff—ours and USG trainers.

Dinner was outstanding. As we reached the dessert phase, I got a nod from the entertainment committee to come backstage. Now, I had already cut the 50 percent check but had to write the final 50 percent. I went backstage, checkbook in hand. And, yes, you guessed it, the Paper Dolls are a drag queen entertainment group. They were a bunch of guys (?) trampling around in heels and hose and makeup but no wigs and no shirts. "Hey, how ya doin'?" asked one guy in a baritone voice as he sucked on a cigarette. "Good—great—looking forward to this," and I really was, having been one of the few in the know. I cut the check, got a firm handshake back, and headed out to watch the fun.

Of course, all the VIPs were on the front row. The show began. They were great! Their lead singer was an alto with a fabulous voice—no lip-synching. The dancing was typical for this genre. They had the snake lady with a real boa who circulated through the VIP table. They got the boss and his boss on stage for an act. It was tremendously fun.

The boss's boss later refused to believe all the folks on the stage were male. Having been backstage, I knew better but let him keep his fantasy.

Moral: Never discount the blending and acceptance of a different culture to outside influences. Many places are, in fact, very open, and that is how you as an international businessperson can establish your relationships necessary for that future business. But always take care of that judgmental attitude!

Offsets—fishing for a better deal.

CHAPTER 4

Dedicated Internationalist
Offsets, Travel Health, More Financial Crises

From Southeast Asia, I returned to the US after almost six years. But I returned by jumping ship to another company. Which brings me to another point on a long-term expatriate assignment. It is my experience (in two assignments) that if you are doing a good job, they will just leave you there. Forget that two- to four-year agreement. In the first place, it takes a year or so to really establish the rapport with the locals. Then another year or so before things are really buzzing. It is often so critical to a company to have their expatriate connected that they will just let you stay until you start foaming at the mouth or quit. While abroad, I paid more than the usual attention to various business articles on the topic. Uniformly, the articles said it is a shame, as the expat is now more than ever a wealth of experience that could benefit the firm. But a succession plan is hard and fraught with risk. Before considering taking that position, carefully check out the history of other expats in the firm. Were they repatriated or did they just stay overseas until retirement? That is not too bad from the age of sixty, but from the age of forty-five, that is a long time away from home.

That said, international assignments do have their perks, such as my master's opportunity, as well as a few others. It is an experience that will be unique. You often get to do or help with almost every job inside a company. Of course, you learn to deal with a new culture in depth. Southeast Asia was my first corporate expatriate international assignment. My first company did not really have a plan to return me to domestic duties; I went back and semi-interviewed with a handful of folks for potential positions but more just to get my name and face back in circulation. My company was at least looking at a succession plan; they even had hired my replacement so we had (for almost the only time in my professional career, Navy included) a real pass down period. But a decent spot back at home remained elusive. There is a high probability that an expat will die, retire, or quit rather than return to the main office. This should be a cautionary note for those considering the overseas assignment. But so often, plans just are not made for proper repatriation—either any at all, or to a position that can benefit from these new and unique experiences. I saw some (though few) successful repatriations at some of my largest companies, but they had the bandwidth and options to offer a returning senior manager or executive.

There is also the issue with the expat him or herself. Many of those going overseas find they like it and have no desire to return to relatively humdrum life in middle America. Most of my contacts from my past have retired from those final overseas positions—often after years overseas. The companies allow this, in my opinion, for a couple of reasons. First and foremost, once trusted relationships have been established in a foreign country or region, they are very hard to transfer or rebuild. It makes business sense to leave the successful expat in place. Furthermore, this trust is only established after several years. I have read you get into your new job's groove within ninety days, as a rule. Not overseas. Allow a year before you are comfortable and your contact roster is starting to grow quickly. And then there are always the financial considerations. Expats cost a lot. Moving them and replacing them is yet another cost. If you can turn a three-year assignment into nine, you save two moves. And, as I know has happened, what if the replacement is a flop? I know of more than one family that did not like the assignment once on station, and they made the breadwinner's life miserable, either locally or by moving back home and just waiting out the tour. I was fortunate in Malaysia, as my first three years were focused in-country, and I was almost always home in the evenings (except for the once a week to Penang)—unlike my neighbor, who covered the region and was lucky to be home once a month. Even in my business-development role, my constrained area brought me back home usually quickly and frequently. Unlike my assignment in the Middle East, where now I was the guy on the plane five to six days a week, returning only to do laundry.

Your Career Is Your Responsibility

There I was ... another night carrier approach to landing in the Indian Ocean. I hated night carrier landings. The inky blackness and the very small, pitching speck of light that you have to approach at over 175 mph was for me, all the time, unnerving. Something called a "ramp strike" has ended many a Navy pilot's career. This is where you hit the back of the ship during landing and destroy yourself and the plane while barely denting the ship.

On this particular night, it was dark, but the conditions weren't all that worse than normal. I was heading down, carrier in sight, working my instruments very hard before transitioning to the visual cuing system known colloquially as the mirror (used to be a real mirror—was now a series of lights and specialty lenses). This mirror showed you whether you were above, on, or below glide slope—that is, in the proper position to land on a carrier. A minute out, you have a reasonably wide band for "proper." But as you cross the lethal back of the carrier, the bandwidth of the proper was eighteen inches in width.

I was actually having a good start to the final approach. This was to be my two hundredth arrested landing on the *Midway*, and I had prebriefed my back-seater that if I felt good, he was to call, "Switchbox 202, Double Centurion Ball!" If I was not bullish, he'd just make the normal ball call (that is, aircraft call sign and fuel state). I felt good, and he called in the Double Centurion attempt. As I got close in, I saw myself going a little high—at the same time the landing signal officer called for a little "right for lineup"; it could mean going slightly right to remain aligned with the deck, but it was also code for dumping a little altitude with a wing-waggle (a trait common to the Phantom). Next thing I knew, the ball had dropped to the bottom of the mirror, and the landing officer was yelling "Power, power, power!" Well, with my skittishness, I didn't need to hear more than one *power* before I went into full afterburner. Good thing. I later watched the landing tape (all landings are recorded), and my plane flew down the length of the landing area with maybe three feet to spare. My relatively new back-seater asked during that pass, "Are we supposed to be this low?" "Hell no!"

I heard later that the air boss called an "all safe" with the words "Double Centurion Ball, Centurion Wave-off." Even my radar technicians below decks but in the back of the ship dove under their desks as they watched me fly by. My second try was "a little high all the way to the three-wire." I was glad to be on deck. The landing signal officer handling me that night was from an aircraft with no afterburner. So, it did not occur to him in the moment of crisis to call for that power setting. (He should have yelled, "Burner!") However, it was probably my use of afterburner that kept me and my back-seater from a disaster.

Moral: It is up to you to manage your career. From avoiding corruption, to remaining inside export regulations, to keeping tabs with your home office as you roam the world. No one cares about you as much as you. As I tell my son every time I leave him (he is also a Navy pilot now), "Don't let the bastards get you killed." So don't let the corporate bastards get you fired!

No time to get sick, either. Fortunately, I generally have had a relatively robust health situation, coupled with an ardent and lifelong exercise routine. However, during my two-plus decades of living and working internationally, I did get seriously ill. In Malaysia, it was a short family vacation to the resort island of Tioman—nowhere near a major city. I got up the first night and had to stay close to the toilet for the rest of the trip. At about two in the morning, I staggered down to reception and asked if there was a doctor. They called in a nice gent—took him about an hour to arrive. He looked me over but really didn't have much he could do; it was clearly a nasty case of food poisoning. He gave me over the course of my stay a couple of shots (called a "jab" in UK English parlance) that got me home. My wife was afraid I wouldn't make it on the flight. She drove me straight to our local doctor, whose wife was also the office nurse. She took one look at me and almost shrieked. After samples were taken and I was lying down with an IV in me, I could hear her yelling at the lab to get the results *now*! The doctor gave me two pint-sized IVs and said if I was not better in twenty-four hours, I would have to check into a hospital.

Fortunately, the rehydration worked, though I did miss my first week of work that I ever have. But that wasn't my first midnight visit to the hotel reception. In Singapore, I came down with such a severe sore throat I could not swallow or talk. They also got a doctor to come to my hotel room with his nurse—at again about two in the morning. He gave me what he could, and within a couple of hours, I was able to swallow slightly. I was there for an airshow, and I missed the next day (and was missed—lots of my colleagues checked on me throughout the day—very nice of them, though they kept waking me up). I felt barely well enough to go to the show the following day, but I still could not talk. With my colleagues, I could write or type on the Blackberry. But I had to give a presentation to a customer. Writing that I couldn't speak, I gave the PowerPoint pitch by writing my comments on a whiteboard beside it.

In the Middle East, I got another nasty case of food poisoning. I was in Riyadh at the time. My local employee and my local rep were meeting with me in my hotel's lounge in the evening. I kept leaving and returning—and apparently growing whiter and whiter. After about an hour of this, they intervened and forced me to go to a local hospital, where I was given enough drugs to make it home to the UAE the next day. Once there, I gave up self-medication and checked myself into the (very nice and new) local hospital. An interesting note on the hospital in Riyadh is that even though I had regional medical insurance and a valid business visa, because I was a foreigner without residency status, they wouldn't take the insurance, and I almost didn't get seen. I also had to pay cash. As I wasn't in the habit of carrying around several hundred dollars, my employee saved the day by paying it immediately for me to reimburse him on a future trip.

As I went through these and other episodes, my medicine chest in my luggage began to grow. Besides the usual aspirin or ibuprofen, I started carrying both Imodium and Pepto-Bismol so I could treat myself in two-hour increments. I also started carrying packets of powdered Pedialyte to pour into water bottles for rehydration. I always had a small container of melatonin—an over-the-counter pill that I initially took to help with jet lag. If you are just exhausted but cannot sleep in the middle of the night for any reason (anxiety, sick, etc.), it also helps. I always had a small number of throat lozenges to help sooth a throat or a cough. And the final item I made sure I had was some kind of antihistamine or decongestant, especially for flights. I was in Korea once getting ready for a sixteen-hour flight to Turkey, and I had a raging head cold and was not looking forward to that. But the airport had a pharmacy. Even though I do not think the pharmacist knew much English, body language was sufficient for him to provide some kind of antihistamine. It was in Korean, and to this day I do not know what it was. But by golly it cleared me up before takeoff and lasted twenty-four hours—a single, small pill. I made sure to keep those handy until they were eventually all used.

In any event, I jumped to another major US defense contractor and returned to a domestic hearth but not a domestic job. It was a good time to return, as the kids were now in middle school and high school, and as exotic as some of the overseas school programs are, in retrospect, we think getting our kids the American high school experience helped not only college applications but also their overall well-roundedness as young adults.

So, back to an international-business-development position and constant travels to Korea, Turkey, Italy, and Australia. Most of these included addressing the subjects of offsets and countertrade. I had not been on the job a month when my boss's boss called me down to his office. "Do you know anything about offset?" he asked. Well, try as I might, I had not been able to distance myself from it completely and had gradually acquired a decent understanding of the basics. This time, though, the big guy needed someone to fill in, as the offset program at that point was a mess (due to circumstances largely beyond the control of the current manager assigned to handle the offset obligation). He asked me to step in, keep the peace, and start planning the recovery. Of course, this would be an additional duty that I would just do on the side of my business-development job. About all I could say was, "Yes, sir." It is time to delve a little deeper into that topic.

Offsets are a form of international trade that is required by a country as a condition of purchase of a company's equipment. Usually it is set forth in policy form, though this can vary widely. As of this book, about eighty countries around the world have an offset policy, and a number of other ones have an informal expectation of some kind of tit for tat in major purchases. While normally associated with defense programs, large civil programs such as a fleet of airliners, major extractive industries, and even power plants and rail systems can see offsets required or requested, either formally or informally.

There are a wide variety of offset types. In fact, offset projects are limited only by the imagination of the provider and the policy limits of the recipient. I know of projects ranging from true barter of agricultural goods, to full assembly of fighter aircraft, to sending a citizen into space. Offset generally falls into one of two broad categories: direct and indirect. Direct offset is that which is performed on the project at hand. Perhaps a local company does final assembly of a tank or plane under contract to the prime contractor. Or perhaps the local steel mill gets an order for all the rails for a subway system. Training on the purchased system, whether in manufacture or in maintenance, is often an accepted offset project.

Don't Bid against a Local If You Can Help It

There I was ... helping the offset manager again. Some offset credit bookings are easy—low-hanging fruit. Others are hard negotiations. This is an example of a hard one to negotiate.

On this particular direct offset program, the overall offset program proposal had been a suggestion, not a commitment, except to final credit target—that is, the proposed projects were concepts, not guaranteed projects. Since the program ran over a number of years, specific offset proposals came and went; after an initial flurry of activity (and credit), the pace of credit accumulation slowed. As the in-country manager, offset was on my to-do list but not at the top. Top of the list was keeping my end user happy via training, spares, and on-site support. But I dutifully helped my offset colleague on his numerous trips in-country to help close out the obligation. To be frank, the fact that the offset program was not in stone on day one was a both a benefit and an albatross to both parties. As time passed, some of the originally proposed projects were no longer viable for the company, and some of them were no longer desired by the country; therefore, the flexibility was nice. But not having set projects (and completion schedules) meant an open-ended potential, leaving both sides hanging as new offset projects were proposed and negotiated. Of course, we still had to get to full obligation. Enter the tough sell.

We were proposing a Phase X (two, three, four—can't remember) to an IT-related logistics effort. This series of programs had greatly benefited the end user, who was desirous of seeing another phase. Unfortunately, a major local and well-connected company was bidding flat out for a similar program but countrywide. Hence the penultimate meeting: we wanted $Y for the project upgrade. Regrettably, the same agency also had to award the other countrywide contract. So, after introductions, formalities, and some usual banter back and forth, the studious, relatively senior civil servant asked bluntly, with a steady, half-knowing glance, "Why should I award you $Y for this one-project, one-base program when Company A has offered to do the entire military for only 2.5 times that amount?" That's actually a good question.

Whoa. Regroup time.

My offset colleague is now looking daggers at me for not having prebriefed this potential glitch. And he was right to do so, as I had known vaguely about this other local tender but had not properly considered its impact on our program. So, we retired to his hotel room to strategize. Suddenly offset was moving way up my priority list. To conclude the story, we did get the offset credit. It involved me working behind the scenes with the end user to have a few strings pulled and a few ears bent. Ultimately, the end user was happy; the offset office was a little grumbly but saluted and carried on, as we still had more credit to conclude (which ultimately we did).

Moral: Someone on the ground has to know about any local competition for proposed offset projects. If the country is already investing internally for similar technology or capability, you stand the chance of being co-opted or losing an acceptable cost to credit ratio. Use your company's on-site manager, offset manager, or your local representative or consultant to ferret out potential competition so that you save your time and the customer's not bidding against a domestic effort.

Indirect offset is anything else accepted by a country. It can be investment in a particular industry not related to the purchase. It can be the purchase of domestic products unrelated to the prime contract, even highly technical ones. It can also be unrelated training (say helping a university establish a research laboratory). And finally, it can be just about anything that the country wants or feels it needs to develop its own economy and maintain its sovereignty. Typically, offsets do not become mandated until a contract is fairly large—normally in this case above US$10 million. Some countries start lower; others start higher. But if you are going in with a single proposal in that range, you should be asking the question whether or not an offset policy exists or is expected.

To Throw Stones or Darts?

There I was ... attempting to explain yet again what offsets are and generally how they work to someone not in the know. Imagine that the offset policy is a dartboard. The general reaction is to throw a big enough stone at it, and you will break the policy into small pieces.

This won't work. Remember that the policy is a government policy, not a company desire. Policies do come and go; there are several out there now that are in abeyance while the country either rethinks its policy or tests whether companies will willingly include local firms in contracts. Also, policies change over time, based on past experiences, new information, or even just a new direction of the government for developmental goals. But that all means the concept is here to stay for the foreseeable future.

Enter the smart company. They don't treat the policy as a board to be stoned but as a target that has a bull's-eye to be hit. The game is not a muscular chest-thumping, head-banging complaint about how unfair offset requirements are. It is, rather, a carefully played game based on finesse, strategy, and skill in attempting to hit exactly what the policy wants. As in darts, the first time you toss an offset proposal out there, you are not likely to hit the bull's-eye. But with enough practice, you hit the target often and where the multipliers are (think of the double and triple rings on the dartboard) as well as, ever more frequently, the bull's-eye!

Moral: Offsets are here to stay. Quit throwing your stones and start practicing your darts.

The real rub of offsets is that many policies require up to 100 percent in offset. Meaning, the desire is for the country to be able to tell its citizens that 100 percent of the purchase price of the tank / plane / rail system was countered with work and reinvestment into the country by the contractor. Obviously, this doesn't work out in reality. What happens is that to encourage certain sectors in the economy, investment or work in those sectors by the contractor will gain what is called a multiplier. For every dollar spent or invested, for instance, the contractor may be awarded three or five or even ten dollars of credit. In this manner, a $100 million offset obligation can be satisfied for something in the range of actually $20 million to $30 million of actual work or orders—and generally substantially less.

So, You Think You Are Smarter Than the Average Offset Office

There I was … the new guy in the international group. Yes, I might be the boss, but that doesn't count much when you are new to a group that has mutual histories dating back to hunting mastodons with Clovis point spears. We were in the throes of concluding a long-sought-after international deal. I asked, "So, what is the offset plan?" I got blank looks, then assurances that, as offset had never been mentioned, there was no offset. But I knew, as informally and as poorly publicized as it was, there *was* an offset requirement in this specific country. But I was told "not to worry, got it covered," and, "we don't do offset anyway."

The contract is being inked, when we receive a letter from the country's ministry of finance asking where our offset proposal was.

You cannot wish away an offset requirement, and pretending to be blind to it is the worst way to go. Remember that you are dealing with a sovereign nation, and they rank higher than any company. Just ask Microsoft about their fun in Europe, or any number of companies and their success in China. You are not outsmarting the country by not asking the question and getting a straight answer, in writing. There are lots of instances where offset requirements are waived for very valid reasons. But if you are not holding the Get Out of Offset Free letter, then you are the dupe, not the country. They will lie in wait until the signature is almost complete—then ask for the offset at no change in price. Then what are you going to do? No time to plan, no time to calculate the potential costs and risks, and this deal has to close this quarter, or you are going to be roasted alive by your boss.

Also, I am not a fan of the strategy to offer a "with and without offset" proposal. Several countries decide on each procurement if they want offset or not and ask for a quote to perform it. But they are also trusted to not change their minds once the proposals are on the table. If you offer "with" and "without," the country knows the spread and will want the "without offset" price but "with offset." And note, many countries will not allow a cost item called Offset Program Implementation Costs.

Moral: Think, learn, and plan ahead for offsets. See my website, www.offsetcollaboration.com.

Back to my first years at this new company. New countries brought new cultures and situations. Also, my added role in offsets created new challenges and experiences. No longer was my only customer just the ministry of defense or chief of the air force. Suddenly I had a host of companies, large and small, wanting to get a piece of my time to discuss how they could collaborate with my company. But all this costs somebody money. Most companies will be building in that cost into their proposal. The goal of a country should be to make their offset policy straightforward enough that the costs of implementing it are minimal—a few percentages on the total program cost. I remember one country's chief engineer growling at me (unofficially) that their offset policy had cost the air force three aircraft. That is a specific hint at the overall cost of the offset program. Some countries are beginning to be selective in demanding offsets—best efforts, "we are watching you" kind of policies. They are working relatively well in countries with an existing defense industrial base. The jury is still out on other situations.

So You Think You Are Smarter Than the Average Internationally Experienced Company

There I was ... having multiple exchanges with country policy wonks on offset policy. The prevailing opinion at the time was that offset is a God-given right for countries and therefore, like manna from heaven, should come to them free of charge. After all, the country is a sovereign nation, while the company is just a company and must follow local law or policy, which usually says some version of "offset must be provided free of charge." Also, that new fighter or submarine or tank fleet costs a lot of country funds—and everyone knows the defense contractor is making a killing in profit, and shaving a little off that profit margin for offsets is only fair.

Think again. Defense contractors were not born yesterday. Often their own defense procurement agencies are their toughest customers when it comes to justifying company profits. The defense company knows how to scour the regulations—local or otherwise—for those loopholes to squeeze a little more profit out, and they will cover the costs of an offset program one way or the other, in spite of what your policy says.

In the case of offset requirements, the savvy contractor builds in the cost inside each and every line item: equipment, spares, training, program management, field support ... You name it, it carries a burden (admittedly usually small) that is allocated internally, far from your prying eyes, to fund the offset requirements levied by a country. Now, some countries have publicly announced "no offsets," either temporarily or permanently. Some also advise upfront on a specific procurement whether offset is in or out, and they have a history of not changing their minds, so they can be trusted. In these cases, the competitive contractors pull out the offset levy so as to have the most cost-effective bid. Cost isn't always king, but it frequently is queen, or at minimum the tiebreaker.

If you have an offset policy but choose on a

particular program to waive it, advertise that early in the bid and proposal stage, so companies pull out that cost. If you advertise late but before BAFO (best and final offer), you have a chance of some additional reduction *not* associated with the real BAFO strategy of a company. But fail to implement the offset or address it when it is public, and the company will gleefully take that extra profit straight to the bottom line.

Moral: You might get lucky springing an offset requirement on companies at the last moment, but most companies now know the cost of offset and price it within all the other costs.

As of this book, there has also started to be an increasing realization that offsets costs, and it should be more selectively applied. As there is little published literature on offsets, often the best way to learn (either from a company or country aspect) is to network with the small group that already does them. There are a few organizations, such as the Defense Industry Offset Association and the Global Offset and Countertrade Association, that have meetings at which training is often offered, and during the main conference, knowledgeable speakers discuss offset policies. In Europe, there are also the European Club for Countertrade and Offset, and a German-based group called DKF. Otherwise, you are generally on your own, scanning country offset policies directly and weaving in and out of their offset offices. But in my case, it was fascinating getting to visit and in some cases survey companies in many places around the world. One thing I learned early on is that there is a lot of capability out there in the world. Guess what? A lot of the best machining tools and robots are built outside the US—and not under ITAR or EAR control. So, many countries can buy them. Effective use, of course, becomes the issue. The trick is to find those technology nuggets in a manner that is affordable, high quality, and exportable— that is, some chance that the work can not only be done properly but that the USG will allow you to make the export of the required data. That is not always as easy as it sounds. The earlier F-35/Joint Strike Fighter example is a perfect case for when it is not as easy to get even adequate information to potential bidders in an international program.

Back to Europe. In the end, the program I was on did not go forward. The 2008 financial crisis stopped many of the new procurements that were not international consortia. This was my second rude brush with collapses in the international business environment. The earlier currency crisis in 1997–1998 had started in Southeast Asia and spread mainly to the emerging markets—South Korea, Russia, and Latin America to name a few. The price of oil also dropped almost 60 percent over a two-year period during the crisis. The 2008–2010 worldwide financial crisis and its holdover into the 2010–2013 Eurozone financial crisis found me again heavily or exclusively engaged in international business. These crises put paid to several international pursuits my companies were attempting to bring in. The crises had an impact reducing US domestic procurements; the frustrating part for me was the natural but false hope that those shortfalls would be almost instantaneously replaced with international business. I was fortunate that a few long-sought-after programs actually did materialize—but due strictly to dire security necessities of deployed military units in Southwest Asia. Most countries will not let their soldiers hang out alone these days; either they equip, or they pull out (which is not great news for the US, who will have to shoulder a greater burden in many cases). During these years, I made multiple trips to many points of the globe—Europe, Southeast Asia, Northeast Asia, South Asia, Middle East, and Australia. Customers were polite, interested, and broke. This led indirectly to another parting of the ways and subsequent downsizings by companies.

My final financial crisis was in what was to be my final expatriate tour—this time in the "rich" Middle East. I use quotes, because the common perception of infinite money in that region is wrong. The locals readily admit to more needs than funds allow—many of them social needs. That meant that in my line of work, I wasn't just competing against other defense contractors, or even for a share of the overall defense pie. I was also competing against hospitals, schools, infrastructure, youth employment programs, and a multitude of other efforts to spread the benefits of natural resource extraction throughout an entire country. All the countries in the Middle East walk a fine line between funds dedicated to curtailing internal unrest and funds dedicated to countering external security threats.

During my assignment there, two events drove the area from tough to really tough: the Syrian civil war and the crash of oil prices. The former, of course, generated a huge need for increased security. This was good for business. All the militaries wanted and needed our products. Thousands of kilometers of borders needed to be protected—surveilled 24-7, if possible. Iraq had still not recovered. Daesh exploded. Yemen imploded. All sounds good for the proverbial Merchant of Death, right? Well, think again. Benchmark oil prices when I arrived in 2012 hovered between ninety and a hundred dollars a barrel—higher some months. Lots of funds. But in the late summer of 2014, the bottom fell out of the oil market. In six months, the price had fallen into the fifties and sixties per barrel, and a year on saw the nadir at around thirty-five dollars a barrel. With the entire region planning on oil prices above seventy dollars a barrel for a break-even national budget, procurements in many areas stopped dead. Only the most critical security procurements continued—and with their own forces engaged or supporting entities in two civil wars, some business came my way. Much of it was in the form of "we need it yesterday." This common attribute of international business—work on a program for years, then suddenly the customer wants it *now*—was exacerbated by the security threat and the dramatic drop in funding sources. Even so, I did not make my numbers most of those years. Really tough—and beyond my control (and theirs).

In pursuing business development during part of these periods, I had several opportunities to watch my prime contractor at work and see the shortcomings of not being able to listen well. I would accompany them to a meeting, listen to the same comments from the colonels or generals, and then we would go back to the hotel together to discuss. In many cases—maybe even most cases—their team would talk themselves into what a positive meeting it was and how close we were to getting a contract. Refer back to the need to listen. That is not what I heard. I could read the body language and hear the words so full of qualifiers that I knew we were doomed. No matter how sweet the pot, this country just was not in a position in the near future to afford the program. And, try as I might, a good industrial participation opportunity (a.k.a. offsets) was going to be a tough sell given the technology I was peddling. My local representative and I talked frequently about this in private. At the time, I was toting a new tablet-type PC with a stylus for graphic notes (a present from my wife). One day, we sat down, and he, looking over my shoulder, had me make a visual graph of budget versus time. In it, he had me draw and fill a line with the budget for each of the major committed international programs from which there was no backing down. I stacked program on program, coloring in the graph of the costs versus timeline. After we were through the major ones—some five or six—he took the stylus and drew a horizontal line about a third of the way from the top of the pile. "That's how much money we have. We don't even have the funds for what we are committed to." Ugh. But truth is better than fiction unless you are reading a book. I continued to support my prime and continued to have interesting industry and offset experiences in this country. But I knew my next salary raise and bonus was not going to come because of that sale.

Toto, We Are Not in Kansas Anymore: Different Countries, Different Cultures. A Story.

There I was ... escorting my vice president on a trip specifically to focus on industrial relationships with a major foreign-defense company.

My VP at this time was an experienced, competent, and effective ... female. Don't get me wrong; my mother was one of the first female reporters at *Time* magazine, and not on the fashion page. My class at the

Naval Academy had the first women. My first tactical jet flight instructor was female. And by this point in time, I had had several lady bosses and, in one company, had been asked by some lady colleagues to join the Diversity Council, which subsequently won an award for our efforts.

After a series of lower-level meetings and tours at various facilities, we finally got to the ultimate elephant meeting—their senior VP and mine. As prebriefed, I was to make the initial introductions and then, presumably, slide to the side and let my VP engage at the elephant level to reach an industrial collaboration framework from which we would go forward. We never got there.

From the start, the local VP was aggressive and hostile. He stayed focused on me, pressing for better, bigger, and more work. And he made several references to the fact that a corporate organizational chart in *his* country would absolutely not have "one of those types of individuals" on it (nodding vaguely toward my VP, a female). So, for an hour or so, I got to politely fence wits with one of the most senior individuals in this large and multinational company, while my VP sat quietly beside me. I maintained my cool and got through to an agreement on the framework and what that document should contain.

We left. I was miffed with the insults—verbal and otherwise—that had been thrown at my boss; however, I just kept my thoughts to myself on the ride back to the hotel. To her immense credit and my everlasting gratitude, she could sense the discord inside me, and in the car on the way back to the hotel, she said, basically, "Water off a duck's back. You did an absolutely great job in an incredibly hostile situation. I have trusted you to a great extent roaming the world on your own, but now I trust you implicitly."

Moral: Not all the world is like your little world; culture also impacts business structures and those in them. You must learn to expect the unexpected and handle it with tact and grace—and then, hopefully, the job will get done.

Body language is so important in international business. Polish your shoes for any trip to Northeast Asia, as you will spend a lot of time looking at them, as will your customer. Eye contact is not favored there, hence a lot of looking down … at everyone's shoes. I remember one colleague discussing his negotiation in the region. It was midwinter, and they were in a cold office. The country team came in and opened the windows—no heat. My colleague took off his suit jacket, rolled up his shirt sleeves, and said, "Ready to begin?" The locals couldn't even last an hour. The point was made, and the heat turned back on. Showing the bottom of a shoe in the Middle East—a big no-no! Many Americans like to cross their legs, leaving a shoe hanging out there—ugh! Feet on the floor, please. The locals will appreciate it. Remember the gent who threw a sandal at the president, George Bush Junior, in Iraq—the ultimate insult in that region. Speaking of which, we long ago as a family abandoned shoes in the house a la Japanese style. It causes huge heartburn for our American maintenance companies, though a few do come prepared for booties on shoes. But all of Asia has a "no shoes in the house" policy. Buy some new socks before you go, as you will be showing either the socks or your toes as you visit. Crossed arms—don't do it. Arrogant, huffy, unrelenting—you do not want those epitaphs on your international-business -development tombstone. Welcoming, approachable, trustworthy—much better descriptions for getting the new business and the job done. There are a few good books on body language, and you should read one.

In the countries where we did have a chance of a sale, I was busy trying to do good things, both on the business-development side and on the offset side. This led to many interesting trips, coupled with a lot of jet lag, a bunch of frequent-flier miles, and a few missed holidays. I did spend a Thanksgiving into early December in Korea and had the pleasure of the neighboring Korean church choir serenading the lighting of the hotel's huge Christmas tree. Which is another good point—Korea had radically changed from my Navy days. Except for the bulgogi and soju, it was a new country.

The plus side of so many weekends there was a chance to see a number of sites, my favorites being the DMZ tunnels and the military museum. The North Koreans were and still are always trying to infiltrate South Korea. It is a somewhat sobering exercise to get basic range information on Soviet-era and Chinese artillery pieces and rocket launchers and overlay range rings on a map from the North/South Korean border on the capital of Seoul, where I spent much of my time. A few bored or disgruntled North Korean patriots could turn the entire city into a graveyard with a few button pushes. But this, of course, made South Korea into a great military equipment purchaser and partner.

Know When to Walk Out

There I was … confronted with a hard-nosed end customer and an equally steel-framed prime contractor wanting to grind on one of my proposed offset projects.

A brief digression. Training as a form of offset is generally a good bet. It may not bring top multipliers, but if you are the representative of an advanced company, almost everything your firm knows is a leg up for a developing country, even a newly industrialized one. Don't *give* it away; *negotiate* it away. The costs are relatively straightforward—airfare plus man-weeks (or woman-weeks—most [but not all] countries don't care) plus some printed presentations and reproduced policies, drawings, software, and other material.

Anyway, we were knee deep in an urgent effort by the prime contractor to conclude the offset proposal, so that check in the box was, well, checked. Remember that offset proposals never win a program, but they can sure as heck lose one if you can't get viable programs on the table. My prime counterpart was losing his hair, getting fat, and going pale from stress compounded by a lack of exercise and sunlight and too many hotel club-lounge drinks while trying to get the deal concluded before the other parts of the massive proposal were printed and left on the desk of the customer procurement agency.

Enter my training program offer. Ignore the spares orders, contracts for touch-labor locally on the product, and other direct offset projects I had lined up. They had mostly all been accepted. To the training. Any good offset office never takes any proposal at face value, and the really sharp ones start grinding on training projects in particular. How do you justify the value? Grind, grind, grind.

We bantered back and forth on expertise developed from decades in the business, intellectual property being irretrievably passed along, and the value of real engineers doing the hands-on training. Finally, at a tense moment, my prime counterpart called a contractor time-out and asked me to step out for a contractor conference. Once we were in the hallway, he started to show a quiet smile. He asked about the weather, my family, and we chitchatted about folks we mutually knew. Then he winked and said, "We had to step out to look serious. Let me do the concluding discussion." Back in we go. After another half hour or so, an agreement is reached on the value.

As I briefed my boss a week or so later, his only comment was, "Why can't we get those kinds of multipliers on *all* our offset proposals?"

Moral: If you haven't read a book on negotiating, do so. Rule number one, of course, is to have a BAFO (best and final offer) set up … and not offer it first. But rule number nearly next is be prepared to walk as a ploy—even if just outside the office. No one but you will know if you are bluffing or really in a bind on the negotiation. Remember the country offset office also wants a successful conclusion so they are not the long pole in a procurement tent.

I did actually walk out once in a negotiation—and made a real-world phone call to the boss. We were on the edge of an agreement. I knew what his answer would be, but I had to have him say so, as the cut that was proposed to make the deal happen was beyond my authority. Sure enough, I got the go, returned to the office, and shook hands—a really big program for my company and a really good feeling for me. Anyway, following my own advice, I made sure to visit several places in Korea beyond the DMZ. The military museum is excellent, if you are into that subject. The scale model of a turtle boat (an armored galley/sailboat used for several centuries starting in the 1400s) was wonderful. Also, South Korea very carefully honors all the countries that came to its aid during the Korean War—a bit moving for me, as my father was one of those who came from the US. The local palace is also a great walking tour; allow several hours. And the hill across from where I frequently stayed—Namsam Park—gives a spectacular view of the city. I have even jogged to its top on the weekend, though I was a bit younger then.

Fun Stuff You Get to Do in Offset

There I was … supporting as a major partner on a huge proposal. I had been wearing both offset and business-development hats for a week or so in-country but stayed on primarily for the offset part, as negotiations were ramping up, and the prime wanted an offset suit collar to grab if/as needed.

We had a good couple of days of various discussions with the offset committee. Sometimes I was in the meeting, sometimes kicking my heels in the hall outside as the prime discussed various proposals to which I was not privy. At the end of the final day was the dutiful summary with the offset committee. At this meeting, to the committee chair's obvious satisfaction, those of us (small group) on the contractor side were invited to a dinner sanctioned by the local department of defense's ethics committee and hosted by the offset committee as a token of their esteem for our hard work. Well, you don't turn down a free meal, especially if the customer is buying!

I met up with my prime contractor buddies prior to dinner for a few drinks, during which—in a relaxed mood—the topic turned to favorite foods. I admitted that most fish and shellfish were not on my list; I was more of a cow-and-chicken man. But drinks done, off we went to meet our hosts.

The location was the largest wet market in the country. That means—you guessed it—fish. We took about thirty minutes to ooh and aah over an incredibly large and varied sample of fresh seafood of every imaginable creature: octopus, squid, sea cucumber, crabs (all sizes and shapes), jellyfish (no touchee until cooked), and big fish, little fish, red fish, blue fish. Then upstairs to a very quaint, very local restaurant. We started with the cutest little crabs—chilled. We ate them like peanuts with the shell on. Then followed a constant array of wonderfully raw or steamed or grilled or otherwise prepared seafood delicacies—a small portion of all the previously mentioned species from the market, all washed down with copious amounts of the local hooch, which helped my aching knees and back, as we were seated traditionally, which meant flat on the floor. (A common place to sit for dinner in Northeast Asia. Some newer restaurants accommodate the American by having a cut-out below the low table but not this one.) It was truly a great evening and an unforgettable one.

We headed back to the hotel after thanking our hosts for a great evening. When we were finally in private, my colleagues said, "Wow, we thought you didn't like fish! But you ate like there was no food for tomorrow! Did we hear incorrectly?" To which I replied, "In business development, you always like what the customer likes!"

Moral: Good relationships with your prime go a long way to a successful program. Even better is a good relationship with your customer's offset committee—a relationship usually built on hard work, hard negotiation, patience, and ultimately trust. And fish can be good for you if not deep-fried and covered in tartar sauce.

I eventually transitioned out of both offsets and pure international business and into a business-development role that was about seventy/thirty domestic and international. But with most of the real program in the US, my focus had to be there. I did start supporting my replacements in the offset roles as I could, and of course I did not entirely escape being the offset answer man for my new boss. But we were focused on the domestic US market; the international trips were there just to keep some of the interest alive.

Multilingual

There I was … another business dinner—this time in four languages.

I was fluent in German, of course, and I had a smattering of French, but my Turkish was abysmal and limited to "good day" and "thank you." But for the upcoming evening dinner, I had to be at my sharpest.

We were hosting a senior Turkish industrialist and politician with a potential view for industrial collaboration. He spoke only French and Turkish. Across from me sat a retired Turkish army general, who spoke only Turkish and German, and our representative who, I believe, spoke Turkish and English and had a decent smattering of French. Next to me sat two company colleagues, one of whom was monolingual (i.e., English only) and the other who spoke English and French. Now began the dinner.

I had a delightful time conversing in German with the general. But, of course, I had to include my colleagues and translate what he was saying or asking. Then I had to translate back. For the politician, we had to frequently double translate—Turkish via French or vice versa. The same for my monolingual colleague— either French or German into English and reverse. It was a good thing Turkish wine is quite palatable; we needed it. We were in something like a thousand-year-old fortress-turned-restaurant. It was a delightful, if exhausting, evening of staying on one's toes and keeping the communication going forward.

Moral: You don't have to know every language ever spoken, but you should learn at least one foreign tongue. Even if not your local country's specialty, it shows you have made that vital first step to being an internationalist.

All good things to come to an end, hopefully with something better to follow. I again jumped ship, this time back to a pure international-business-development position. Some of my customers were now old faces—Australia, Italy, and Korea. But I did get to start working Sweden seriously and dallying a bit in India and a few other places. Also, about this time, I started my doctoral studies. This is another good lesson on maintaining close contacts as you roam the globe. One of my classmates from Malaysia had been sent by the government to the UK to get her doctorate with a focus on offsets. We stayed in touch, and occasionally I was used as a sounding board for industry inputs to her research. She introduced me one day to her thesis advisor. He knew my background and said he was sure I could delve right into the doctoral studies without the need for master's-level coursework (since I had two masters already). As my travel was ramping up and the kids were growing old enough to fend for themselves, my wife suggested I take him up on that. Thus began a five-year journey that took me with reasonable frequency to the UK's military college, Cranfield, and to several other countries for fieldwork on the effectiveness of offsets. The research was challenging, especially getting hard data. But with the explosion of the internet, I was able— from anywhere in the world—to access the Cranfield library, find articles and papers, and even order books. I did have to learn a bit how to work within the British educational system, but that went well in the end. And what I learned definitely impacted my view on offset implementation.

Technology Transfer and Education

There I was … in Upstate New York?

Learning is a challenging thing. Yet, to get ahead, one has to learn. For a country to get ahead, its population has to learn. Yet history is rife with of all sorts of descriptions inhibiting or even prohibiting learning. From Spain and Portugal who suppressed, via the Inquisition, academics in astronomy and navigation a century *after* these two disciplines had so effectively launched their world empires, to the reversals of China and the Islamic Caliphates to stop or even destroy learning and invention in their areas (e.g., clocks, iron smelting, and in the case of China, any oceangoing vessels). All of these out of fear that the populous would get out of control and demand more say in life. Yet few would argue that life five centuries ago was better off than it is today—after all those years of learning and technological improvement. This clinging to the past and fear of the future is also still alive in the modern world.

In offset, you have to seek out as many connections as possible in case your target country wants a particular product or service. This led me via odd connections to visit a town in Upstate New York. I was invited to visit a company in a technology incubator in the hopes that I could use them as a potential offset project. What I recall is that the incubator itself was located in an old textile-manufacturing facility that was being converted, building by massive building, to house small technology start-ups. The town itself was struggling through a revival. The recommended hotel was, to be polite, *dated* but comfortable. Small restaurants and shops were opening, but you could tell from the streets and sidewalks that public infrastructure was a victim of the town's current depression. The discussions and demonstrations went well, but the fascinating part was the over-lunch chat about their new office and how that came about.

Turns out in the late 1940s just after World War Two, the State University of New York (SUNY) decided to reorganize and to expand its campuses to provide better opportunities for New York residents. SUNY sent out interview teams to a number of upstate cities looking for the best options. One group came to this town. However, the town fathers were knee deep in a textile boom caused by the war and its aftermath on worldwide industries. They could barely keep up. The mills were running at breakneck speed, as were profits. The last thing the local leadership wanted was to have its workforce start educating itself at the collegiate level, as that meant (in their minds) the workers would move on to other better jobs, causing a manpower crunch. So, this town went out of its way to discourage the SUNY interview team. SUNY selected other towns for expansion campuses.

Yet within twenty years, the return of peaceful trade resulted in India, Southeast Asia, and Central America becoming the world leaders in textile manufacturing due to their much lower cost of manpower. The New York textile industry shrank continuously from the mid-1950s until it was virtually extinct. The textile mill buildings then became abandoned relics, and the town almost dried up completely. By the 2000s, the new city fathers began crafting a vision that included campus extensions, tax breaks, and subsidized facilities (e.g., the reworked textile buildings) to attract information and electronics technology start-up firms. Results at the time of my visit were still in limbo, but the one redone textile factory was already filled with a dozen tech start-ups, and work had begun on the next building over.

Moral: Local culture has an impact on technology transfer. The impact is nontrivial and must be included in the calculations of both the recipient (government and industry) and the provider.

This is exactly why countries often value the transfer of technology above all else. It has to be relevant technology. It should also be focused in a specific area or a few areas—not every technology all the time. Lack of focus leads to lack of critical mass (read John Porter's *Competitive Advantage of Nations*—dated but still true). And the country has to be able to absorb the technology. All these have key issues. But the policy goal is to create in the local economy a viable increase in capabilities and capacities to eventually allow their local companies to compete directly in the world market or enter into the supply chains of major multinational firms.

Of course, the real trick is attempting to value the technology being transferred. This is not a straightforward process. It relies on several factors: what is currently available in-country; what is internationally recognized as state of the art; and what is actually being transferred in terms of skills, certifications, and transportability of the skill set to export work or domestic substitution. Sometimes this can be easy, such as simple purchases from an already existing and viable subcontractor. But others are much harder to evaluate, especially as designated "technology transfer." In this type of program, the supplying company wants offset credits for training or transfers of drawings, software code, and general know-how to a domestic entity that did not have that knowledge before. There are various ways to attempt to measure, such as the cost of development of the original project, the market value for either the product to be made or the value of royalties to be waived, intellectual patents and other property, the potential for future exports, and a hybrid of these items. But what all of these generally lead to is extensive negotiations until such time as both the supplier and recipient (country) offset managers have to conclude a deal ... or not. Some companies, especially smaller ones, just do not have the wherewithal to work up offset programs and choose not to bid. At other times, the main program itself is not considered sufficiently large or technologically advanced for a country's office to demand the offset, so they waive it.

The quantification of a Coca-Cola production license or a McDonald's food chain is relatively straightforward, as it is consumer oriented and based on the number of locals able to afford the purchase of such items. But the transfer of sophisticated goods in defense or other significant civil infrastructure is much harder to quantify. Will the country be able to actually absorb the necessary skills to perform the maintenance on the systems? Will the approved technology transfers assist local companies in exporting more product? These are the great unknowns in offset theory and practice. Valuation can come from a number of sources. However, it is best assessed by the benefit to a local company (or group of companies). The two major factors are cost avoidance (i.e., doing the job internally in the country) and export (i.e., skills that allow for greater value in the export arena). It is critical that the country understand its own local capabilities and enable its companies to go forward with the transferred technologies—either as the local champion for support or at an increased export capability.

While researching all around the world, I was also still doing my business-development job. But more and more, I was seeing a blend between the job and the research. Countries could almost always be convinced to give me or my guys a hearing. But—at least the meetings I was in—they all wanted to know what kind of work was in it for their local industry. That is, the days of the quick sale appeared to be fading and not just in one geographical market. More and more, countries were targeting the global supply chain of major companies to help create a sustainable production line for their local companies. This is a complex task and requires the locals to be also internationally focused for long-term results.

*Corruption these days: not negotiable! Listen to your
guiding angel, not your tempting devil.*

CHAPTER 5

Abroad Again in a Dynamic Area
Setting Up Offices, Corruption, Yet More Cultures

Company downsizing caught up with me, and I was in the job-hunt mode. One of my contacts in a previous company who had left earlier for greener pastures in another, smaller company saw my LinkedIn change and called me immediately. This company needed a director to be based in Abu Dhabi, United Arab Emirates. Would I be interested? I apparently was the easiest interview my new boss had. He said later he had conducted twenty-five or twenty-six and all bogged down on the issue of moving overseas. I just said, "Not a problem. Treat me fair, and we'll get along just fine." He kept his part of the bargain. Off I went to the Middle East. My first day on the job was in Dubai at the annual regional business-development meeting. I didn't get a company badge or computer until two weeks later when, after house hunting, I finally made it to the company headquarters. That is where I began to learn what I had really signed up for. The Middle East had been historically one of the most important markets, and I was tasked to expand it as much as I could.

Definition of Warranty

There I was … managing a demanding customer in the Middle East. Warranty was often the topic of discussion. What constitutes an under-warranty repair? Tire tracks across the top of a crushed device would not normally top my list. But that is exactly what we honored.

It seems that such a device had been returned a year or so before my arrival. We, of course, indicated that the warranty did not extend to being driven over by an armored car. We learned not too long later that the poor enlisted guy who had turned it in was sentenced to three months in prison for damaging expensive government property.

Up comes a new idea: fault-free warranty.

We offered the customer an extension on their warranty period inclusive of a no-excuses clause that amounted really to new replacement units per contract period (usually a couple of years). This the customer gladly put under contract. So, for the first few tire-track-damaged units, no harm, no foul. And they did not come in all that often.

Moral: You can find business opportunities by molding your business model to take advantage of a country's culture to the mutual benefit of both parties.

Different cultures work in different ways. For instance, in my office building in Southeast Asia, the office buildings would shut off the air-conditioning between about six at night and eight in the morning. I would be an early arrival in my office, and it would be warm-ish and humid. As soon as the AC kicked on, things were fine except for the occasional roll of stamps or self-sealing envelopes that all stuck together due to the overnight humidity. (This also happened to me in the Navy, in training in Pensacola, Florida, when the officers' quarters' air-conditioning failed one day. Everything that had a lick-to-seal requirement had to be pitched.) This didn't work as well up at our on-base repair facility.

Air-Conditioning Dilemmas

There I was ... trying to explain the need to keep the power-hungry air-conditioning units running 24-7. The first statement from the customer was, "Why do you need so much AC?" After we explained all the computers needed to run the facility, they installed the appropriate AC system. In fact, they redid the base electrical system, because we were now drawing more power than the neighboring town. But now came the training/culture indoctrination part.

First, they turned off the AC every evening. This caused condensation to settle on all the electronics: the repair stations themselves and equipment to be repaired. Water plus electronics equals bad. So, we got them to stop turning off the AC. But then we would find them with the windows open during the day. Cold plus humidity equals water condensation, which is bad. Finally, the poor locals doing the repairs settled into the fact they had to wear jackets while doing their job.

Moral: In dealing with different cultures, you need to see the big picture of the requirements and the implementations and how they will interact. This is particularly true of technology transfer as an offset project. A culturally effective transfer will often be a lasting transfer.

Back in region after the trip to the headquarters and another major company facility, I had to start learning all the cultures. I had experienced that in East Asia. With by now extensive experience in six of the countries there and visits to another three, I had found more different than alike between them once I got past the big picture of calling them East Asia. I found that experience similar to what I was now learning in the Arabian Peninsula. No two countries in the region have exactly the same culture; each has its own personality. I even found that in the Arabic language, which I made a woeful attempt to try to learn at least verbally. I had two of my local staff almost come to blows over the proper translation of portions of some documents. And with staff at one time from four different Arabic-speaking countries, I found it rare that all four (if all together) would agree on one interpretation. I even found it impossible to use a Dubai, UAE-based firm to translate Saudi government documents; I had to have our Saudi lawyer (who was on retainer) translate a crucial contract phrase and then call my US lawyer to explain why it was okay. Business-development guy to corporate lawyer, no dice; but Saudi lawyer to American lawyer, we got corporate agreement.

SAGs and NAGs

There I was ... watching the Tom Hanks movie *Hologram for the King* for the fifth time before sending it off to staff in another office; if you haven't seen it, you need to. With the new local leadership in several of the Middle East countries, a lot is changing. I am literally agog at what I am reading in the news and hearing from colleagues that is going on, like women driving and public cinemas. But for my years in the region, it rang true on multiple levels in multiple places.

I spent over half my time on the road, which is why I had a serviced apartment in the UAE. I was never there to clean it and only barely had time to do laundry and buy the limited groceries I needed. For the first year and a half in one country, I had a delightful local working for me in Saudi Arabia. His downfall was being too Western and too local at the same time. In any event, he gave me some great times and introduced me to NAGs and SAGs.

Remember this is in the Middle East where multiple countries restrict or outright ban alcohol. NAGs were the Non-Alcoholic Group. We met late at night (I'd swear serious business is only conducted after midnight in the region) over lamb, tea, coffee, a few roasted vegetables, and rice. Sitting late at night, we would chat about just about anything that their English and mine would withstand (my Arabic being limited to giving directions to get back to my hotel with the taxi driver).

SAGs were the Strictly Alcoholic Group—on a closed compound or in a country not so strict so as not to get harassed. Full bar! Still the lamb and rice at midnight. But they'd send me back with a water bottle full of rum or vodka. So much for saving my liver by living in the Middle East.

Moral: You will find subcultures in almost every culture. Tread carefully when you have to walk on both sides of a narrow cultural line.

One way to learn a region is to travel it alone. It is generally also the hardest way, especially if language barriers exist, as they have been frequently in my East and Southwest Asian assignments. Having a reputable representative can, therefore, become critical. He or she may be local—so you are technically alone—but as they usually have a tremendous grasp of English (and in my case Americanisms) and stay close to you the entire time, you are not really alone.

Know When to Get off the Train

So, there I was … coming back from a visit to a prominent company in a semioffset role.

My goal had been to pitch the art of the possible for collaborative research/production for a high-technology product. It had been an interesting meeting. I spoke in English, then waited while my representative translated. The potential customer was very engaged. It finally became apparent they knew a lot of English, but they just were too embarrassed to use it. But with my relaxed and open demeanor, they relaxed during the course of a couple of hours, and we finally got to the intriguing situation where I would speak, no translation needed, and they would respond to my rep, who would translate for me. Nice time-saver.

Anyway, the meeting was as positive as could be hoped for in the situation, and my rep and I headed back to the train for a return trip to the main city and his home and my hotel. Ah, the gentle rocking on a train after a long day and intense meeting. As we clattered along at a good clip, I nodded off. I woke up just as we were pulling into a station I recognized as close to where my hotel was—problem: no rep but the rep's briefcase! In a just-awake panic, I hopped off the train with the briefcase, thinking he had also left but forgot his briefcase. It dawned on me in the taxi to the hotel that I had probably screwed up, as instead of a five-buck ride, it was more like twenty-five. Sure enough, it was not long after getting to the hotel that I got a panic call from my rep about where the heck I was and where was his briefcase. He had just gone to the toilet as we pulled into the stop … one stop before we were to get off! (He did come by the hotel to collect the briefcase.)

Moral: Yes, your rep needs a sense of humor when dealing with an American. And this was in a country I actually knew well, having worked it extensively in a prior job. Prebrief all legs of the trip so you don't make yourself look like an idiot and scare the bejesus out of your local rep.

Selecting a good representative is one of the hardest tasks you will have to accomplish. A good start is the US Commercial Service. They have diplomats in many of the countries around the world that keep a database of potential representatives vetted at least at the first stage. If you buy into their Gold Key Matchmaking Service program, they will also add in local market research, arrange meetings, and accompany you on those meetings when you arrive. There is a cost, but it is not prohibitive and is based on company size. My next favorite way to find a rep is to check with the local American Chamber of Commerce. They are company neutral, are often staffed by an American and some locals with extensive local business knowledge, and they can usually give you a few points of contact. Don't overlook the fact that your home state might have an overseas office. Maryland has eighteen overseas offices, for example, as well as funding to help a small business go global. Finally, never forget to network, either in your industry or with anyone you know already doing business in a target country. You cannot obviously go to a direct competitor, but you can look one-off. Reps do more than just translate and network. They teach you the culture and the local political quirks, and even help you plan your offset program if required. Having a rep alongside simplifies many things. An example follows, where my buddy had a rep to help get the equipment *in*, while I did not to get it *out*.

Recovering Demo Equipment

There I was ... heading to a town in southern Saudi Arabia. There are always two hard parts of demonstrations—getting the equipment to the site and picking it up from the site. When it is a local demonstration, the two get combined, and it merely makes for a very long day. But when the demo is remote, you start facing lots of transport and customs issues.

A good colleague and buddy had arranged for a demo in southern Saudi Arabia. I had watched him try to remotely guide the equipment into the desired town—a fiasco. The equipment kept getting bumped because the baggage of the locally inbound labor force would fill the cargo hold and not allow room for paid freight. You need to check in to a flight in the Middle East at a holiday time to appreciate that. Families would have literally dozens of bags—sometimes even a big-screen TV or a large stereo set—all gifts for relatives back home. As an American businessman with frequent-flier status, I would take my one or two little bags and circumvent the check-in with little problem. But it was easy to see why our equipment would be bumped, even on the inbound flight to southern Saudi Arabia. But finally the gear arrived, and my buddy and our local representative got it set up at an air base for testing. They left the gear there for a month of testing as part of the deal.

Enter my good deal. My buddy called me one day and asked if, per chance, I could go down and retrieve all this kit. Ugh. Sure, but it will cost you. So off I fly from my office in UAE to southern Saudi Arabia. Fortunately, as he had been there, he had a recommended car rental company and hotel. Unfortunately, the largest vehicle they had at the car company was a Mercury Marquis. With a bit of help from Google Maps, I got to the base. After an hour of kicking my heels, I was told I was at the wrong gate and to go to a different gate. After getting there, I had the smallest staff sergeant available to help retrieve the gear. What I had not realized was that the demo kit was on top of the air traffic control tower. Elevator to floor three; climb up stairs to floor four; take a pull-down ladder to the roof. This gear weighed collectively over five hundred pounds.

I disassembled the setup and—using a borrowed, frayed nylon rope—lowered each piece of expensive gear down the ladder to the fourth floor. Then the sergeant and I manhandled it to the third and stuffed it in the boxes. Note to self—check for number of boxes before filling them. It took me forever to figure out how to stuff everything into six boxes. At the very end, I noticed a label that said, "One of Seven." I spoke no Arabic, the sergeant spoke no English, and the officer who was remotely helping by cell phone now didn't answer. But I made it clear we had to go back up.

The sergeant was not happy at all but did return with me to the tower. Sure enough, we found box number seven hiding under a desk on the fourth floor; then all the equipment fit snug as a bug. Now we had to stuff this gear into the Mercury: trunk full to overflowing and tied shut; boxes filled the back and passenger seats; I was crunched as far forward as the steering wheel allowed. I gave the sergeant the biggest tip I could. I drove to the hotel for the night and arrived sweaty and exhausted. Fortunately, they took huge pity on me and agreed to serve as a staging area for the equipment until the shipping company would collect it (in three days). But now I had to manhandle all the boxes—with the help of a luggage cart and an elevator, at least—up to the office. Once there, it made a man-high pile of shipping crates that covered one wall.

Moral: As the Lone Ranger, you will have multiple tasks to do for the company overseas. Try to enjoy the variety as best you are able.

That small tip, by the way, might have been an example of an expediting payment, one of the few allowed by US law (though in this case, it really was more of a tip than a payment). While back at the headquarters, I also got the usual briefs now on company policy, ITAR, and the Foreign Corrupt Practices Act (FCPA). The last was something that directly impacted my predecessor and would in a residual manner impact me and my staff's relationships with our US office for my entire tour overseas.

The Grand World Tour

There I was ... reading in disbelief the Security and Exchange Commission's filings on my company that had generated the opening that I filled. Dribs and drabs had come out over the several years I was overseas but not the complete story—for good reason, as it was certainly a legal matter, and it was a true lapse of judgment on the part of several folks I knew, at least in passing.

It is not uncommon for some countries to ask for the costs of factory inspections to be included in the contract. This protects them in a couple of ways. First, the funds are locked up in an obligated line item, so safe from their own budget cuts. The second is that if the factory inspection is a failure, they are not out any additional funds to return for a future inspection. In this particular event, the planning got out of control largely due to local culture. The local employee on the scene took it upon himself to get the team to and from the US inspection site. This was not unusual, and with other staff being pulled a hundred ways, their initial thoughts had to have been, *Thank heavens, he is covering it.*

Except the trip went from origin to a stop in the Middle East to a stop in North Africa to Paris, to New York (staying a couple of days at each location), and only finally ending at the factory location for the on-site inspection, where the visitors stayed less than half a day. Then back via London and on to a final intermediary stop and then home. Oh, and each member of the team was given a gold Rolex as a gift. This, dear reader, is way, way beyond the bounds of prudence. Even so, the whole thing might have blown over with a fired employee and a small fine. Instead, once the travel receipts were submitted, a cover-up was attempted—to no avail. Now heads rolled up the management chain several levels, and the position opened that I eventually filled.

The company eventually settled in a double-digit million-dollar fine and a program to revamp its FCPA education program. While no guilt was ever admitted, a few of the individual players also settled with the SEC for substantial financial fines. It certainly made my life more difficult, as now I was the director of the region, and every move we made came under the closest scrutiny due to past experience.

Moral: FCPA is not a line to be crossed. Once crossed, the consequences are dire and long-term. Keep eyes open, including on your subordinates. Failure to know is not an excuse.

The US has long had anticorruption laws, for instance dating back to the Security Exchange Commission law of 1934. However, in the 1980s, in response to a few egregious cases, the FCPA was beefed up and broken out. It took almost a decade to really gain steam, but as the new millennium dawned, record numbers of cases were bringing record-breaking fines and compliance agreements, and not just to US companies. Using the SEC connection, any company listed in the US, or acquiring a subsidiary listed in the US, could be brought under FCPA jurisdiction. Companies in many fields have been held accountable: oil and gas, mining, defense, power plants, even IT. For a number of years, Europe lagged in implementing anticorruption laws (or at least in enforcing them), but as European firms acquired US subsidiaries or wanted to enter the US market, many of those laws were finally beefed up or enforced.

Bribery and Other Stories

There I was … again presenting an essay on international security to my master's class in Malaysia.

I had just presented my final paper. I cannot now even recall what the subject was. But the follow-on question and answer was open book and had nothing to do with the paper I had just presented. After almost a year in the course, I had gained the grudging acceptance of two dozen ladies and gentlemen of non-American, non-European extraction. They jokingly called me The

Hegemon and accused me of working for the CIA. They apparently had coordinated the question they wanted to ask: "What corruption have you experienced as a defense contractor in our country?"

Whoa. What a question. And, yes, I could answer it, under Chatham House Rules. First, none directly—except getting stopped by the police for an illegal U-turn. My bad, a "Hard or easy?" from the officer, and a few hundred of the local currency fixed it expeditiously with a glare from the officer not to do that again. And my boss and two company colleagues in the car were laughing almost until they cried. Ugh.

One story heard on the streets—Russians selling equipment of high value. The potential representative asked what the commission would be. "Twenty percent." "Twenty percent?" was the local's reply. The Russian response, misunderstanding the reaction, was, "We can pay more."

But the next answer was more sobering. I was approached by two individuals to be a representative for a particular product. As we politely discussed the topic in my office, I indicated that the maximum I could arrange for a representation fee would be 7–9 percent of sales price; asked was 15–20 percent. We parted amiably but with no agreement. The next day, one of the two called and said they'd be happy for a midrange on my offer. I signed that individual up.

Next story—again heard on the streets but with more corroborative evidence. A European firm had landed a major order. The rep asked, as was apparently within his rights, for all the commission up front: 10 percent of a multibillion-dollar deal. The Europeans were aghast; they had not made an arrangement in their contract with the rep for pay-as-we-get-paid (a standard clause). But ... it was not entirely corrupt. The rep was a major connected political figure. He was going to pay 90+ percent of his receipts directly into the local party coffers to help the elections planned for a couple of months' hence. Yes, he made a bit of money, but most of those funds went to supporting luncheon and dinner parties and speaking engagements of local supporters of the leading political party.

Just think of him as a private political action committee and lobbyist but with no public reporting requirements.

Moral: You are in the front line of protecting not only yourself but also your company from FCPA allegations. You need to be careful at all times, and just because the other lemmings are jumping into the sea does not mean you should follow suit.

For a company, it is essential that a culture of anticorruption flows from the top down. Employees should not only get the annual training, but they should see management living it and feel that to break the rules will not be tolerated. As one cartoon shows it, an old manager with a younger colleague is looking closely at a chart labeled Offset and Corruption, with a line drawn between the two words. The old manager is saying, "That looks like a fine line between the two; what say we just ignore it." You do so at your own peril.

Lawyer Interviews

I got a call one day from my boss. A corporate lawyer, whose job included due diligence on representatives and internationally based company personnel, was making his biennial trip to Southeast Asia. He was not a friend. He didn't feel he had done his job if he hadn't terminated a representative or gotten an employee fired. My reply, "Got it."

At the time, I was managing several representatives in Malaysia and Thailand. I called the Malaysian reps directly and advised that they might be contacted. One of them was a new lady. I made a point of saying, "Yes-and-no answers only—no detail. Be honest but curt." Sure enough, he picked two of the three, including the lady. Of course, he talked to me. He had the gall to ask if the lady had offered sexual services to get the position. He asked about all the others, with that friendly *wink and nod—trust me* body language. He apparently asked her the same thing. What a snake. Anyway, my Malaysian reps and I cleared the hurdle for this trip.

My problem was one of my Thai reps. A number of months prior—five or six at least—he had called me up to go visit a squadron that had some maintenance issues. The location was some three or four hours north of Bangkok (though, given the miserable traffic in that city, that might not have been too far out of town). We left early and got there in good order. The entire trip up, he harangued me about how my hair wasn't combed (I never comb), while his was slicked back clean with Vitalis. My shirt wasn't starched (ironed but not starched), while his was. My tie wasn't perfect (though it had Navy wings, unlike his). My fingernails were not manicured. And so on.

Into the meeting we walked. I chatted for over an hour with the commanding general, partly in English and partly with translation assistance. Then we had lunch at the officers' mess with the general and his staff. The rep and I departed back for Bangkok. The rep was in disbelief. I had pulled off one of the best meetings he had ever attended with a senior commander and an American. He said the words in Thai, the body language, and all other aspects of the meeting were outstanding. And I did it looking like a ragamuffin, in his opinion (he even made me wet down my hair in the bathroom before the meeting). What this guy didn't get was that by being prior military and by being open and honest, rapport was quickly established. My task was to ensure better support for this squadron, and that I knew would be possible.

On the long drive back to Bangkok, the rep starts relating stories on how he does business. Some were innocuous—nice company giveaways like a manicure set (that he made sure I got and that I still have). Others got well into that gray area that makes folks subject to the Foreign Corrupt Practices Act very, very nervous. He made spiritual donations to local temples on the behalf of officers. He helped get their children into US colleges by pulling a few strings. In the end, I had to tell him, "This conversation never happened, and don't ever, ever repeat it." He was, again, shocked and said, "It is just the way business is done in Thailand."

So, fast-forward the five or six months. The rep's father has died, and he was up-country for the funeral. The lawyer agreed to drive the four or five hours up to conduct the interview. I had told the rep the same thing I told the Malaysians: be honest but be as short as reasonable and stick, if possible, to yes-and-no answers; do not embellish or provide additional information not requested. I awoke the next morning to an email from the legal team saying cease and desist all contact with that Thai rep. So, I expected—and received—a call from him that morning after he had read his email about being terminated. He sounded terribly hurt. I asked how the visit had gone from his viewpoint. He said it had gone great—that the lawyer had been so nice and so polite that he felt like a friend. I asked the rep if he had repeated any of the discussion we had had in the drive back from my visit to the military base with him, and he said yes. Terminated, just as I had predicted. I'm lucky the lawyer didn't figure out I had heard it first.

Moral: Culturally acceptable overseas may not be considered legal in the US. Try to help your representatives and locally hired staff to understand this in a meaningful way.

Some folks are just hard to coach. It is a special problem if that person is on your team—a local with a different view of what is acceptable. As my earlier story on the world tour indicated, that can really get you into trouble. I had to carefully watch my local staff to keep them on the straight and narrow. This is hard enough for Americans pressured to close that deal. But for the locals, it can be just crazy. We are all trained to think that the customer is always right, and we should accommodate. But if what the customer wants to bust FCPA guidelines? It is time to walk away. And that can be emotionally hard to do.

Locals That Don't Exist

There I was ... attempting to bring on a new representative in the Middle East. My company had a vigorous vetting process. Email questionnaires, phone interviews, and even visits to local facilities. Enter a "strong recommendation" suddenly from an existing customer that we should use Company X as a local representative ... as the deal is about to be inked. Stinks. But we will give it a go.

We asked to meet the principals of the company, and they came by my boss's hotel. The meeting didn't go well. I arrived late due to other business and was able to hear only the final exchanges. To go further, we requested a follow-on interview between our legal department and the representative's legal group. This task fell to me as the regional director. But for some reason, we never could get the representative to agree to the call. We moved to plan B—an on-site inspection by a third-party entity vetted for assessing the reality of a company. Amazingly enough, that also never happened. All the red flags were flying:

- Sudden introduction of a representative as the deal was at closure.
- Representative was of a different nationality than the country to be under contract.
- Representative could not or would not present a local brick-and-mortar office to meet at.
- Commission, while admissible, was high—more than a few percent—for such a late engagement and for which they (apparently) had not contributed to.

The worst part was dealing with my local employee who was frantic and emotional about getting the representative on board because the local customer had requested it. Hence, an issue—after multiple discussions, my local employee really did not internalize why this whole deal smelled bad to our legal department. Fast-forward several years: no deal, no business for a couple of years; then we find the recommended representative is now on the outs. Fast-forward a bit more, and this country resumed purchases from my company, because they needed the technology and equipment. No rep.

Moral: You need to keep your staff in line with regulations. Resisting what seems an easy path to close a deal will cause local anguish but save you (and them) in the long run.

On the other hand, there is often manna from the gods that falls into your plate. For instance, I had a representative in Southeast Asia who had made a lot of money helping sell cargo aircraft to the local military. I asked how that had happened. "Manna from the gods." Basically, this country was getting close to ending its fiscal year, and it had a large trade surplus to spend on necessary infrastructure. The decision was made to immediately procure these cargo aircraft, as they would benefit the entire nation: disaster relief, movement of supplies, participation in international peacekeeping missions. The government, therefore, logically called in the representative of the appropriate company and asked for a quote "yesterday." Off the rep went, got the quote, presented the quote, got the contract, and off to the races with the aircraft. However, when it came time to pay the representative, the company lawyers were very, very suspicious. Fortunately, the representative had all the paperwork on hand for review and analysis. Yes, they were making a lot of money in a short time. But, yes, the country wanted these aircraft and wanted them *now*. So, the audit conducted by the producing company satisfied everyone that there was nothing going on under the table for the order.

Regrettably, this contrasted with a representative I had a decade or so later in the Middle East. The gent was excellent at relationships, and his family had a couple of real manufacturing facilities. Unfortunately, when it came time to renew his agreement with associated thorough review of his records, he had none, or they were a hopeless mess. My company even sent an accountant over an attempt to sort it out and help set up the backbone of a reliable system. But not having kept track of all his expenses, he was unable to flesh out the actuality of his business expenses. He was terminated due to his poor record keeping, which meant an inability of our company to adequately vouch that the payments had not been used in a manner that violated FCPA. This would hurt us financially for a bit as we went to find another representative. But it had to be done, and management had made the proper decision in spite of how painful it was and how sorry those of us who worked with the representative were to see him go.

Finally, a few more fun things I did on this assignment. The first was to complete my doctorate; the second was to open an office for the company in Abu Dhabi and set up a subsidiary.

During this overseas assignment, I finally finished my doctoral thesis on the long-term effectiveness of offsets. I had made trips on my own dime to Finland, Switzerland, and Malaysia. Unfortunately, my advisor thought my data too thin on the first two (though I did learn a lot about their experiences), so I returned yet again to Malaysia with a greater focus. It was with some reluctance that my advisor finally let me call it quits, submit the final thesis for review, and go for the thesis defense. I won't say that was a cakewalk, but the two gentlemen reviewing me made the process as easy as could be done. Partway into the hour and a half, one blurted out, "Well, you know you are getting a pass, don't you?" No, I didn't; my advisor had set my expectations very low. But I didn't say that, and I tried not to smirk. After the grilling, I left the room for twenty or so minutes, and I was then called back in with the official results—some modifications and clarifications but a total pass once that was complete. We then all went to the local college's officers' club for lunch, where the first thing the two reviewers asked me was, "Now tell us how it *really* works in defense offsets!" As I drove with my advisor to the campus exit, preparing to leave and saying a final goodbye, he said, "I can't believe it! That was one of the best defenses I have ever had a student conduct!" Chalk one up for business-development skills.

Another fun thing I did was a bit of travel. Some was exotic, some more exciting than I needed, and some ... delegated. You have probably seen the *Mission Impossible: Ghost Protocol* sandstorm. Yes, dear reader, that really does happen. I was driving with my wife down from Abu Dhabi to Muscat on a vacation. We had overnighted in Al Ain (a delightful city filled with forts and museums) and were across the border headed toward Oman's capital when a storm hit. I didn't see it too often, but I did see it more than once in the region—an OMG here comes the dust, then the wind, then the rain, then total blackout via a driving sandstorm. We had to pull over and wait it out. I saw the same thing twice in Abu Dhabi and once in Riyadh—an impressive show of force of Mother Nature's power.

Some other fun experiences follow: I tried to share the regional advantages and disadvantages with my local staff. That was easy when traveling to Oman or Qatar or Jordan. But the big money was elsewhere—primarily Saudi Arabia. After losing my Saudi national employee, I hired a retired US Army colonel to move to the kingdom and be my man on the ground for work there. He had in his past been based years in the kingdom and knew the ropes. I happened to hire him out of a UAE assignment, but that was just the way things went. Of course, not long after hiring, I had to let him spread his wings—by throwing him out the window. Not a very good mother bird, am I?

Delegation: Jeddah or Paris?

There I was … Jeddah or Paris? Some choices are harder than others. For instance, Jeddah or Paris in June? Paris was for the Le Bouget Air Show; Jeddah was for a presentation to royal security—partway into the humid Arabian summer on the coast. I had been there once in the past on a similar briefing mission, and that suit went straight to the dry cleaners on returning. I had just hired a veteran Saudi expert, but he had only been in the company a couple of months and was still learning the equipment specifications. I was already scheduled to support the company at the Paris air show—flights and rooms booked. Two days before I was to depart, I got a panic call from my Saudi representative. They absolutely needed someone to support a senior government meeting in Jeddah within forty-eight hours.

So, this is the good part about being the boss. I created a PowerPoint slide deck and talked it through a couple of times with my new guy. Then I was off to Paris, while he was off to Jeddah. The poor guy. To make matters worse, our usually outstanding travel agent had accidently booked him on a plane change in Medina. Non-Muslims are not even allowed to exit the plane in Medina. He eventually got to Jeddah, gave the pitch the following day, and returned exhausted to his home, then still in Abu Dhabi. I, on the other hand, toasted his excellent performance in absentia at the Paris air show. It became a standing joke between us—I would go to Paris, while he would go to Jeddah. A great guy and a thrill and an honor to have worked with him (he departed after a couple of years for a truly better offer).

Moral #1: It is good to be the boss.

Moral #2: A career in international business slots will lead you to many diverse places. By your retirement, Jeddah and Paris both will be just two small pins on your worldwide travel been-there-done-that map.

During my tenure in Malaysia, I moved offices twice. It did involve finding a location and then working with a designer and contractor to set up the new facilities. Though it was time-consuming, it wasn't really all that difficult in the end. However, in Abu Dhabi, I was tasked with setting up a full subsidiary from scratch under UAE law. That ended up being a pain, and not all due to the UAE. Over the course of the two years it took me to accomplish this, the company shared plenty of responsibility for the delays and issues I had to gradually surmount. The root cause was a need to get real Abu Dhabi residency visas so we could proceed to get military base clearances for my field engineers. We were all there on Dubai Free Trade Zone residency visas. All legitimate, but base security refused to extend more than an occasional week's pass to get on base—and on base is where most of our customers were. Also, there is more than a little bit of competitive rivalry between Abu Dhabi and Dubai, so having a Dubai Free Trade Zone–issued visa always generated some good-natured but pointed remarks from the military in Abu Dhabi. Hence, a couple of years into my assignment, the boss directed me to go figure out how to set up a full Abu Dhabi subsidiary rather than mooching off our Dubai Free Trade Zone depot entity.

In the battle of wits to see where the new UAE entity would be reporting, it recalled to mind my many brushes with corporate mergers. This is because my current company was trying to decide where the new UAE entity should report. I had been part of a merger. On the way to Malaysia, there was an announcement that my current company was being bought by another, larger company. This led ultimately to some very interesting conversations. For instance, the buyer team often felt that the bought team was really in control. "They bought us with our own money!" Turns out the feeling was mutual. "Pampered pets" was my former company's opinion. As the defense guy in Malaysia, I often got a bye in the vindictive flowing between the original company and the acquiring company; much of this was at the biennial air shows in the region, which forced both the old and new folks together. But I remember being visited by the business-development expert on the civil side, who said, and I quote, "You should close this office. We do not want you here in this country." Now, I hardly ever got a call related to the civilian side of the new corporation. But this gent refused to be inclusive and was even more paranoid when I was directed to start using his well-connected local representative as part of my representative constellation. I remember the initial discussion with that rep. He was dismissive of me. It was then I learned the value of discussing your family prior to real business. I looked young for my age (at that point). He assumed I was some thirty-something, inexperienced, fair-haired favorite child of some bigwig. In fact, I was older than he was; mentioning my children's ages is what brought the matter to the forefront. He could not believe that I was the senior company defense representative in-country at the time, and as far as I could tell, he never released that resentment. Not long after, we did merge with another company acquisition, and a colleague joined me who looked much more age appropriate for the part (and he had a much better golf game).

Back to mergers, I played nice with both sides and was rewarded. But as to mergers, many of the rank and file never get over it. On joining my next major company, I quickly learned I was part of the old acquisition of several years prior—and not to forget it. Pins, coffee placeholders, even a few banners with the old company name were still prominently displayed. Both internally to that group and externally with other entities and acquisitions, those in the trenches hunkered down and refused to release their old memorabilia. On arriving at yet another contractor, I found a similar resentment. Those folks in Town X (our assigned sector headquarters) didn't understand our business—partly because my division chose to tell those in the headquarters as little as possible about it. Even in my final major company, who had finished acquisitions a decade before I arrived, I could easily detect the disdain that the West Coast had for East Coast—and vice versa. And that was not to mention the overseas acquisitions and associated assimilation difficulties.

Many of these mergers were the result of the end of the Cold War and subsequent shrinkage of the US defense industry, and specifically a 1993 meeting now known in the defense lexicon as the Last Supper, where the deputy secretary of defense told a group of senior executives they needed to merge, concentrate, and downsize. When I had joined my first civilian employer in 1987, for instance, they employed approximately 130,000 folks and were growing. By 1996, when another company bought/merged with them, we had shrunk to about fifty-six thousand. It was a traumatic time, during which I was lucky enough to stay in and blind enough not to jump ship like many of my slightly younger and highly skilled coworkers. I had a sobering visualization of this in the early 2000s at yet another company's training session (a "work better together" class). The entire class was asked to go stand under placards that read 0–5, 6–10, and so on, in five-year increments to 35+. My new company had taken a "don't fire when possible, but don't hire unless critical" philosophy. Now, the question was, "How long have you been here?" I was in the 0–5 category because I was new. All the others under my card were two decades younger. The sobering part was the gap between us and the cards over fifteen years. Almost no one was in the intervening decade. Above fifteen years were packed most of the class under each card, and even the 35+ had a good grouping. All in all, a presidential report in 2000 found that over six hundred thousand aerospace workers alone had exited the industry in the decade after the end of the Cold War—and they weren't counting land and naval systems reductions. Europe, by the way, was similarly impacted. Anyway, this may partially explain the angst at the worker level in every merged company I worked in. Good luck to management on that topic.

Returning to the UAE office incorporation, setting up in any UAE free trade zone is easy—no local partner, just fill the paperwork, rent a facility, put some money in a local bank, and you are in. Chartering a subsidiary in an actual Emirate is far more complex. To start, you need a local partner. They can usually be a silent partner (paid annually to remain silent), but you have to have their company and their signatures on the incorporation documents. The first glitch was, therefore, switching partners midselection. After going with our local lawyers with one gent for several months, the price went up, and the lawyers said they'd find someone else. Several months wasted. Then we had to have a proper company headquarters' board resolution created, signed, translated, attested, and reviewed by UAE offices. This took months and months due to decisions about how an internal corporate entity would incorporate and therefore be controlled for tax purposes for the Abu Dhabi office. It seems that the simple solution, reporting back to the head office, was out. In the end, the head US office delegated the task to the subsidiary in the UK, which decided to place us under the subsidiary in Belgium. This was all fine enough, except it greatly increased the paperwork that had to be approved at each board of directors' level. To top that off, the paperwork arrived at the Belgium office just as the summer holidays started, and no progress was made for six weeks due to the summer holidays (I really want to work for a European company next time). Then came the requirement to have it translated into Arabic, something that took some time and was only to be done by an authorized translator. Then those documents had to be signed by Belgium in the appropriate blanks before returning to me, along with a power of attorney for me to sign—which also had to be translated. Over a year after my initial direction to incorporate and set up an office, we finally trooped into a certification office in Abu Dhabi with an expeditor hired on the recommendation of our local legal counsel. While waiting interminably to be called in, the expeditor came over and sat beside me with a frown. He quietly said that the person to whom we had been assigned was a pain and had too many complaints about all the documents he examined. The expeditor's guess was "failure." Sure enough, after being called in and sitting politely while a fifteen- to twenty-minute exchange in Arabic occurred, we left without the approval. But the expeditor had a thought. Would I be able to meet him at a different office late that afternoon? I said yes. We met about as late as you could be at another office, got a friendlier reviewer, and left with the approved document.

They Are Trying to Kill You with Food

There I was ... another roasted lamb.

Make no mistake about it, the Arabs are some of the friendliest folks when you are on their side or are their guest. It does not matter what country in the Middle East—once you are adopted, you are doomed to great food and mountains of it.

The issue is a constant case of attempted murder via overfeeding. I thought Americans loved to overeat. But the Arabs take it to a fine art—dozens of mezza dishes of hummus, tabbouleh and other salads, shawarma, and mains of grilled or roasted lamb, beef, and (or) chicken, all with a delightful, fresh-cooked pita bread.

Now, you may think you can do this—but think again! As the honored guest, you get first pick. The savvier locals will help you. But you have to dig into the dishes with your (right!) hand. It is an art to cup the fingers correctly to get that great mix of rice, lamb, and spices. Then you get the honor (as the guest) of having food thrown at you—well, not exactly but as a measure of respect; if one of the other local eaters gets a particularly juicy piece of meat, they will toss it in front of you. And you have to eat it! Hence my stance that they are trying to kill you with kindness by making you overeat! The good news is that much of the food is lean—low fat. But quantity—whoa!

So, a Texan talking here, prepare for juicy, salty, and peppery but not spicy. You can make an Arab sweat by just showing him a jalapeno and threatening an eat-off. While savory, Arabic is not spicy, with one exception: single trip—maybe an anomaly ... Yemen. There, even my Thai-loving American colleague (if you don't know, Thai has got to rank as one of the hottest/spiciest cuisines) admitted that the lunch we had was finally registering on his Thai-spiced-damaged taste buds. Our only nervousness was the plethora of AK-47s with the general's bodyguards.

Moral: International business is not a "fly in, go to the hotel, go to the meeting, go back to the hotel, and go home" business. Expect—even look forward—to experiencing the differences. For a true internationalist, they are almost always enjoyable.

I thought all of that would be the hard part, but it was just the beginning. I now had to set up the banking details with the help of both the US and UK offices. The company had a worldwide agreement with a major international bank, so that was their choice. It was not the bank of choice for any company I knew in the UAE. It took me forever to unravel why, but it turns out that, specific to the UAE, this bank—competent as they were for much of the world—would not or could not comply with all the various local banking requirements. Even more inconveniently, the only place I could meet with them to work on this was their Dubai office, not the Abu Dhabi branch just up the road. It took months to establish the two required accounts. And this is where the four signatures came in. Everyone in finance above me hated the thought that I, a business-development director, had to be on the list of signers. I already had delegated spending authority beyond the amounts in the two bank accounts, but they did not want me to be signatory on any checks from these two smaller accounts. They finally had to bend to the inevitable, but more months were lost on that internal negotiation. I guess they figured I would misuse the local equivalent of about $15,000 in each account. I promptly set up an agreement with my direct financial overseers to report any check I had to write. I finally ended up with the two accounts and authority to sign the checks. I was also given the power of attorney to rent the office space. I always sent all paperwork copies back to one of the higher offices. At least the UK office reviewed it promptly.

For the lease, I got permission to hire a real estate agent to help my workload. For several months, we would meet maybe twice a month and hit two or three properties. I would critique them, she would take notes, and back to the search. I think she finally found the perfect spot—that or I saw a huge For Rent sign off a building that would work and had her check it for me. For our purposes, it was ideal (we wanted an outside porch several stories above ground level for our equipment to test and demonstrate in the office). It was a stripped-out office, which is usual—at least overseas: on departure, you are to rip out everything to the concrete. After a couple of quotes, I found my local outfitting partner and started forwarding plans to my boss for layout approval. This became a moving target. This was exactly during the time of internal company reorganization. I was not only adding previously approved staff (a couple of folks) but was about to absorb another division's staff into my domain. What started as a comfortable four-person office with work area and conference room soon ballooned to eight plus two hangers-on from the old division not assigned to me but working closely with me. To keep the conference room and workshop, we now crammed in only two offices (one guest/mini–conference room) and ten cubicles. The poor build-out guy was bringing me new designs practically every month for four or five months and wondering if I would ever sign a contract.

But sign we did sign, and after over two years of planning, the first hammers fell, and screwdrivers turned. I won't cover all the technical details of that, but suffice to say it took three months, and in that time, I got to learn how to register a business phone and internet system— not one phone call, about five office visits in person—and as I was the only authorized signatory, my true job—business development—I had to offload heavily on the staff. I also had to turn on the power and water (more visits in person, though fewer than the phone system), and I had to throw out the server we bought because the company IT wonks weighed in (late). To get access back to the US on a company-encrypted line, we needed a different and far larger server. And on and on. This divided evenly between the usual bureaucracy of a foreign nation and the usual bureaucracy of a large company—all working to slow us down. We finally had electrical power, lights, and air-conditioning and actually had our first group meetings (though on folding chairs and tables). In fact, the furniture had only just started to arrive at the four-month mark for our first official meeting: a company-mandated, in-person FCPA refresher briefing by our local lawyers. Go figure. It had been a standing joke by my boss—how hard can this be? (He knew full well.) In the end, we only had one major glitch, which was a lesson learned:

Hacked

There I was ... dealing with my office outfitter. He kept asking why he wasn't getting paid his first 50 percent.

I kept checking, and my folks assured me he had been paid. I had numerous emails and finally got a series of documents together and compared the accounts. The money had been wired to the wrong account! The finance office stoutly denied that and produced an email directing the wire to the new account. It was a hacked email. It *looked* really close to the proper email, and the attached document *looked* close to the original invoice. But someone had intercepted the outfitter's email, doctored the invoice to a different bank, and made off with $25,000. The bank was in the UK, so I called my counterparts there. I then learned that this was a common scam and there was no way to recover it. In fact, we were lucky to be only out that amount, as sometimes the hackers get into real estate transactions and make off with ten or twenty times that amount.

This had partially come about because I actually took some vacation time—at precisely the time the hackers started substituting documents. Since I was on vacation, I was not paying close attention. And since I was on vacation, the finance folks politely decided not to ask me to verify. Once I had sorted out the mess, we had a three-way verification phone call: me and the outfitter in my office, finance in the US. This time, the money made it.

To conclude the tale, a couple of minor wires got through after this, but the large final payment also got hacked. Fortunately, I was not on vacation and was paying very close attention and intercepted the note. We did another three-way call to verify the final payment.

Moral: Unfortunately, you are often the best defense for the corporation while overseas. Spam and phishing attacks are commonplace, and even the best corporations can be duped. Watch that email address closely.

The final chore I had to face was now transitioning my visa and those of my staff to the Abu Dhabi residency visa. I did have the help of our lawyer's staff, but I also had numerous informal offers on this to "help expedite." My boss said the lawyers were expensive enough and to stick with them. As the president, I had to get mine first. So that meant first cancelling my Dubai visa, then submitting all the forms—usually translated—to the proper office. What was supposed to take two to four weeks didn't. There never seemed to be enough paper to satisfy the local visa office. I started by checking with the lawyer's staff weekly, then biweekly, then every other day, and in the end daily. I finally directly inserted myself into the calls with the visa office and fortunately had a gent at that office take pity on me and my current situation. As we went through all the paperwork, there was some number that was wrong on my form. As he dug deeper on his end, he said I had a number, but it was a different number. He gave me that number, and I redid all the paperwork, and voila! Visa! The bank had been using an incorrect number the entire time and had not bothered to dig into the situation. After two and a half months and two trips out of the country, my new visa could go forward. The two trips were because I had had to cancel my existing Dubai visa; therefore, I had to leave the country every thirty days to renew my temporary visa. Fortunately, I traveled constantly for business, so no harm, no foul in a sense. But what agony—and why the lawyer's staffer could not figure that out remains a mystery to me. Regrettably, a separate moral: Sometimes if you want something done right, you have to do it yourself, or at least be very personally involved with the local support.

Charting my own course.

CHAPTER 6

Charting a New Course
Visas, Self-Employment, Future of International Business

After five years in the Middle East, I felt it was time to come home. Actually, I began to feel that way at about three years—but as I mentioned earlier, companies are loathed to repatriate a successful expat. I didn't have it as bad as a friend in a different company who showed up in Saudi Arabia a couple of years before I got there and was still there a couple of years after I left. But still—time to come back to home and the boat (too expensive to ship to Abu Dhabi—I checked). Also, I was gradually desensitizing myself to the local environment and going to ever more dubious places for potential business—Northern Iraq (Kurdistan), Yemen (at least before the civil war broke out), the Oman/Yemen border, and Lebanon (Bekaa Valley for a demo). Yes—time to get back where my biggest danger was while driving to the gym or grocery store.

Irbil

There I was … into Iraq finally.

"I'll go if you go." Famous words from a really good colleague and friend. I mean, it's not like it's Baghdad and the Green Zone. So, to support a representative who wanted my colleague's kit, I said yes. That's the NAFOD (no apparent fear of death) working again. Except it is Irbil and not as dangerous as billed. For example, their airport is newly reconditioned, and I was there to sell surveillance equipment to keep it even safer. My partner was there to sell explosive detection devices. It was a modernizing, comfortable city with extensive security where we are staying. My companion was most nervous when they collected the luggage at the hotel for extra screening and he had to let them haul it to the lobby. We were accompanied only by a single car, and personal weapons were there but not obvious. There was even a modest nightlife.

My buddy won the business. I merely had to accompany him another time for training (he was a great instructor). My division was less successful. We performed an outstanding demonstration on a separate trip—in the middle of the Kurd/Daesh fight and therefore with no funds to buy the equipment. Irbil has an impressive old town—a World Heritage Site but in need of rehabilitation. They are working on it, but with almost all your population out to war, the progress is slow. Hopefully with the recent collapse of Daesh, progress will resume.

Moral: International-business-development managers overseas should be willing to help all parts of the corporation. You never know when the favor will be returned, even if only drinks at the next bar.

My time in the Middle East was at a serious conjunction of security issues. That is why I was there—take advantage of the situation and sell. It sounds a little mercenary, but I was not a gunrunner like in the movies *Lord of War* or *War Dogs*. The equipment was sophisticated and usually ITAR controlled. There were no fly-by-night deals. In fact, the specter of US regulation and inspection and the general misunderstanding of the purpose and effect of the multitude of US export documents generally inhibited, or at least hampered, business for my company. But business we did, in multiple countries, every year. The US was still heavily engaged in

Iraq and Afghanistan; in fact, to support those efforts is the entire reason my company had established a depot in a Dubai free trade zone—ease of access. During my tenure in the region, Syria fell apart into civil war, and that war spilled into Lebanon, Jordan, Iraq, and Turkey with both its own fight and the rise of Daesh. The Arab Spring occurred throughout the region. Border issues and even clashes were common. Iran was threatening the US as much as it could. And ultimately, Yemen melted down into its own civil war.

I went twice to a conference the US Fifth Fleet (based in Bahrain) hosted every eighteen months or so on mine/countermine warfare and border/coastal protection. The stories and challenges facing the region were almost mind-numbing. However, they were also apparently not unlike other border issues worldwide. There were people, drugs, booze, and weapons crisscrossing the borders. I did learn, to my surprise, that among the most smuggled items in the region was, seasonally, charcoal and goats. It sounded odd, but for the holy Muslim month of Ramadan and especially the holy holiday Eid that follows, you needed goats to roast, and charcoal to roast them, and the local supplies of most countries had trouble keeping up. Hence the black market; the charcoal and goats would be hidden under legitimate cargo in the bowls of the dhows that plied the region largely unregulated. Much of it came from Africa, and with the Somali piracy on the wane due to the presence of the multinational patrol fleet, business was back up.

This and other events demonstrate the issues of selling (or in the government's case, gifting) equipment to less stable areas of the world. My company's equipment was already in country in several uses as part of attempts to shore up the security situation there—which I think has been dicey since the time of King Solomon's rule. In the past century, they have hardly known peace: Ottomans were driven out after World War One, there was a brief border war with Saudi Arabia in the 1920s, there was the British occupation as a colony not long thereafter until independence in the 1950s led to a decades-long civil war until the 1990s. This reunion did not last long at all, with a return to partial or total civil war by the mid-1990s. A period of modest stability resulted in increased international investment (such as the port of Aden) and security assistance—all of which collapsed again into new protests, repression, and finally another full-blown civil war in 2015. It was in early 2015 that the above story occurred. We and our partner had high hopes for assisted security assistance for their military. Alas, that withered on the vine.

Yemen was not the only place our equipment went orphaned. There were still units in Iraq in need of support and repair. My more reputable representatives were on the lookout for our equipment so they could step in as the intermediary for repair or replacement. Also, much of the equipment could be gifted or left behind as US forces downsized or withdrew (depending, of course, on the technology involved). This is viable business for a representative if you have a government stable enough to pay its bills. We also had serious interest from Lebanon. Unfortunately, its delicate situation made direct exports and deep engagement difficult. Nonetheless, the US and Europe were helping as they could, and we had ever-hopeful representation that this would lead to future business.

Bekah Valley

There I was ... about to witness normalcy in a civil war—an oxymoron. I'd been to Irbil in Iraq twice since Daesh grew. Now I was being asked to send an engineer to the Bekah Valley in Lebanon, and he was understandably reluctant.

I had been to Beirut several times at the requests of my representatives. It is a lovely city mostly recovered from its terrible civil war in the 1980s and has some of the greatest food and prettiest women in the Middle East. However, the compromise government, split between Christian, Druze, and two Muslim sects, Shi'a and Sunni, all still have issues, and the Hezbollah remain as a threat to folks like me—especially since they happen to control the areas around the international airport. I always held my breath taking a taxi or hotel car between the airport and my hotel in the Christian sector. Now I'd been asked to go support a demonstration in the Bekah Valley, hard up against Syria, which was raging a ferocious civil war that had several times spilled over into this very valley; Hezbollah had been sending fighters to help the regime at the behest of Iran.

Anyway, potential business is potential business, so I suited up (well, polo shirt and khakis) and said I'd accompany my engineer. This was becoming a NAFOD habit (no apparent fear of death) that was making my wife understandably nervous. Equipment shipped and cleared customs, and off we went by truck and sedan to an air force base in the heart of the Bekah. My contact was also an American—and remarkably, a fellow alumnus—who had lived a decade plus in Beirut. He had successfully hosted me on several occasions, so I had a great degree of trust. This trip proved that out. We arrived early in the valley and visited an ancient archaeological site as well as a renowned vineyard before the demonstration for the Lebanese Air Force. Almost no one else was at either place except for some Beirut-based folks bringing adventurous out-of-town visitors. The base expected us but was still unprepared. Equipment was set, but the demo was not really going to start until the next day. Secured in the officers' club, I left my engineer and returned to Beirut for meetings the next day with various senior officers. Demo went well, and my engineer (and the equipment) managed to both get out of the country without incident.

The demo almost didn't go at all. There are heavy ITAR restrictions on Lebanon—at least as interpreted by my export compliance staff. While I would point to one paragraph in US law, they would point to another and prevent most equipment from coming. Fortunately, the gear we needed this time had all transferred from Department of State to Department of Commerce jurisdiction. This meant we could demo and even sell, if we could get a contract. The meetings generated a lot of discussion on both this equipment as well as the ITAR-controlled equipment—and how we would go about supporting, training, and maintaining in the face of ITAR restrictions. A good question for the USG, which, at the time, was quietly slipping in copious amounts of material to help the Lebanese armed forces maintain their fight against Syrian intrusions—all legal but all quiet and therefore all unusable information for my internal tussle with my export compliance staff.

Moral: In offsets, you need to know the lines in export compliance and comply. There is no gray area. But you also need to watch for changes and argue on your potential customer's behalf, as they will have no champion but you to solve their desires in technology and work. Again, don't miss a chance to see a part of the country.

I finally found a position outside my current company that returned me to the US. Now all I had to do was extricate myself from the entity that I had established. Winding down my participation in the newly establish Abu Dhabi entity proved daunting. It was mainly due to bureaucracy. As the local president, absolutely everything had my name on it, and almost every scrap of paper for running the office required my signature. I paid all the bills, had the lease with my name on it, was the sole authorizer of resident visas for my guys, and—perhaps worst of all—I was the sole remaining check writer for the two local accounts. Originally set up some two years prior, three of the signatories were in the US, and I was here in Abu Dhabi. By this point, two folks had quit, and the third was now in a position that technically wouldn't allow him to sign these checks. Ugh. I was running between banks and up and down to Dubai (where our main bank branch was) until literally the final day. I am not entirely sure how I would have done it differently, but certainly missing the departure and transfer of three of four signers should have been caught. Something to think about as you consider setting up an overseas office. My departure from Malaysia was much more orderly even though it was quicker by two months because we had all the paperwork in place and my replacement on board.

Wading into New Business

There I was … shoeless, cuffs up, heading to airport security and check-in.

I traveled frequently to the Omani capital of Muscat. It is a lovely city—very low-key in a sense, as it is not crowded with the very high buildings of many of the other Gulf countries. It has retained a picturesque, low, three- to four-story construction painted brilliantly white. It is how I imagine the Middle East must have looked a hundred years ago. I highly recommend it for a visit. The Omanis must rank as one of the friendliest folks in the world.

Anyway, Oman is on the eastern edge of the Arabian Desert. So, flooding is not something that would normally come to my mind. However, it did rain in the mountains seasonally, and when it did, it was a deluge and caused lots of flashfloods. One trip, I was returning home via a local taxi to the airport. Since in Oman many of the Omanis hold a regular job, I had a local driver with virtually no English capability. We tried a few experimental Arabic and English phrases and left it at that.

It had rained overnight. No big deal, I thought, until we got to the airport. They now have a new modern international airport, but at the time, I was headed to the old one. And a lake was in front of it. Not being able to communicate, I watched in both a little bit of anxiety and curiosity as the driver assessed the situation, muttered a number of phrases, and then drove splash-in to the front door. Fortunately for him, the water was just a little below the door's lower lip. I stripped off shoes and socks, rolled my pants up to the knee, and hopped out with my briefcase into calf-deep water. The driver, hitching up his local *dishdash* (typical Arabic gown), pulled my luggage out of the trunk. We both waded almost knee deep to the curb and entrance. He got a big tip.

I went through security barefoot, then walked up to the check-in counter, much to the tittering giggles of the check-in ladies. There I put back on socks and shoes and lowered my cuffs.

Oh well—that happens when a desert gets its annual inch of rain in one hour. You would think that a desert would welcome rain, and it does in moderation. One of my Saudi military contacts was still griping about an answer he picked at a USG language school: "Which of the following is pretty weather? Sunny, rainy, snowy, foggy." He picked "rainy" since it happened so seldom it was a cause for fun. But having experienced deluges in Jordan, Saudi Arabi, Oman, and the UAE, I can say with experience that a deluge is not a welcomed event.

Moral: Adjust to conditions real-time and hope no broken bottles are on the outside of the terminal.

I was a little unfair in the above on the "holding a job" statement. Of course, everyone needs a job, whether an engineer, salesperson, hotel staff, business-development person, politician, or diplomat. But I did find it interesting who I met at the hotels and offices I visited. While not 100 percent, here is the breakout. In Saudi Arabia, Qatar, Kuwait, and the UAE, I hardly ever—in fact, never, that I recall—met a local citizen managing the hotel desk, cleaning the rooms, or doing any tasks below a senior executive level. I know it was a source of exasperation for the leadership, as they were always attempting to come up with ways to entice their locals into the commercial sector, not the government sector. The militaries of both countries had large numbers of local nationals. But they also had expatriate supporting staff, from the tea and cleaning boys, typically from India or Pakistan, to the engineers and contracts negotiators—from almost everywhere, including such far-placed locations as Colombia, South Africa, Malaysia, and the Philippines. Next on the list were the Omanis. I frequently met real Omani nationals running the hotel check-in desk and driving taxis. The military and industry offices still had a number of expatriate support staff but—personal estimate—less than half of the staff. In Jordan, Lebanon, and Irbil, 100 percent of the hotel staff were locals—from check-in staff to cleaners. Same with the government offices. I would occasionally run across a non-Jordanian, but as often as not, he was a subcontracted technical field representative on a specific product. An exception to prove the rule: as I was leaving, on one of my last visits to Amman, I ran across a Filipina on the hotel staff. She was, however, there on a rotational assignment to get a more nuanced international feel before moving to other locations of this very large international hotel chain.

By the way, this does bring up another ITAR gotcha—and it sometimes snuck up even on me. I had not really had to deal with the situation where my customer and my staff were multinational. In Finland and Malaysia and many of the countries I dealt with during the 1990s and 2000s, everyone working on the program, from local industry to the government, were nationals. The license would just state the government, major industry players, our representatives, and our local staff. But in the Middle East, it was a whole different world. As I indicated above, many of the countries utilize experts from many places around the world. Now, I knew our depot had to have a special license for its repair technicians who were not Americans. But it wasn't until we hosted a delegation for a demonstration back at a factory in the US that our export department had one of those OMG moments. One of the experts was not from the subject country and could not be allowed into the building beyond the lobby, or to any meetings. This negative effect then led to a frantic editing of licenses by me to send back to our export department to add a few dozen countries to almost all of our licenses in a half dozen countries. There is no exception to this that I am aware of, and it behooves you, the overseas guy, to know the origins of those working with your ITAR-controlled systems and help the export folks get the correct documents into place.

My departure was due to a little fortune smiling for a bit. The small Australian company that hired me I had known for years (among other reasons, due to repeated attempts to use them as an offset program). They were looking for a US person to staff a business-development position in the US. This position picked up a lot of firsts for me, even thirty years into the business: first time I had worked for a foreign entity; first time I had worked for a privately held company; first time I was working out of my house, not an office. I loved their products, but it always takes a while to develop the rapport, even American to American. After about a year, we parted ways. Unfortunately for them, within a couple of months, the remaining Australian business-development professional with a US focus, a hard charger, was summarily barred from entering the US due to too many days in the US for too many years. This does raise the topic of visas.

Most countries—only most, mind you—give US citizens a visa on arrival, usually good for thirty days. This is fine for your average business trip. But there are countries where it is not so easy. For instance, in my past markets, both India and Saudi Arabia were very important. But you cannot enter either without a visa in advance. That takes preplanning. You need a letter of invitation (there are groups that will help, such as the US-Saudi Arabian Business Council). You have to deliver your passport and fee for processing (there are groups that for a fee will help expedite this, and I highly recommend that). There are many different variants on visas, and the State Department tracks them all on their website. Oman and Jordan—buy on arrival (but in Jordan, only in Jordanian currency cash). Qatar—buy on arrival but only with a credit card—no cash. Irbil and Lebanon—free on arrival to US (different countries often get different visa treatments).

Don't Forget Your Passport

There I was … in a scenic coastal town with glorious weather, about to go see my prime contractor's main facility for the major project I was supporting as both business development and offset manager. Nice jog along the waterfront in the morning, then into the business suit for the leisurely ninety-minute drive to the facility. This was at a joint-use military/civilian facility, so you needed proper identification to get on the base.

Hmmm … you'd like to think your colleagues in international business were not born yesterday. But we all make mistakes. So, after the nice drive to the base, we hop out to get our ID badges, and I am the only one with my trusty passport in my suit pocket. My American colleague had, oops, not brought his, and a US driver's license wasn't going to cut it. So, off they raced back to town to fetch it, while I was left kicking my heels at the main gate.

The guards and the local facility took pity on me, and while my colleagues were racing (and accruing what I understood later to be multiple camera-speeding-tickets), I was given a nice strong cup of joe and a delightful, personal tour of the facility of interest. In fact, I got to see quite a bit more than my now-harried colleague did on his return about two hours later. (Yeah, do the math—ninety minutes each way, but they returned in only 120 minutes. They paid for a few highway patrol salaries on that run!)

Moral: Always carry your passport—wears it out, for sure, but a worn-looking passport makes you look like a salty international businessperson.

Know before you go. And keep track. A friend with a company in the Middle East returned to renew his residency visa one day late. In spite of countless trips over, he forgot he lost a day on the trip, and his residency visa had expired. He got to spend fourteen hours in the airport's police office until he was finally fined and let go. The fine was trivial, but spending fourteen hours with the police after a twenty-hour flight was the real punishment. I do highly recommend a second passport for extensive business travel. A limited-duration one can be issued that allows you to surrender it for in-advance visas while you continue your job. I had all my direct reports get one when overseas. Once a visa is in it, if the visa is longer duration than the passport, the visa will still be accepted on entry—just present both the expired and the new passport. By the way, residency visas (meaning you are going to stay a while) are a whole other animal. It is often necessary to employ a local expeditor to help personally navigate the bureaucracy of most residency visa offices overseas.

Free Vacations

There I was … doing the management thing. While in Malaysia, one of my responsibilities was getting everyone and their family a residency visa and keeping them current. These visas were good for three years.

You had ninety days to get a residency visa approved or you had to leave the country for a couple of days and then return. I used a reputable expeditor (a division of a large, multinational accounting firm) to run the traps for me. I'd hand the passports over with the check and await the return. But frequently the ninety days would be close enough to expiring we had to send folks out for a weekend.

I remember one family of six whose ninety days were finally going to expire. They were up in Penang. So, I had them booked down to Kuala Lumpur, where I personally met them at the airport to hand over the passports so they could leave—in this case for Singapore. The wife was thrilled. Here they are in exotic Malaysia, and the company is already sending them for a free weekend in Singapore! I sent folks variously to Thailand, Indonesia, and several times to Singapore.

Me? My visas always got back within the allotted period. Maybe because I was the local boss? Anyway, my wife grumbled about that several times—missing out on the free shopping trips to Singapore. (She got her share of shopping trips to Singapore, at my expense.)

Moral: Treat your folks well by planning ahead and accommodating. International assignments can be a boon but will also be stressful.

This is something that your US office will not understand unless they have been in an expatriate position—why couldn't I get a visa as easily as I get a passport. Different country, you are not a citizen, their rules. It also applies to longer-term stays. In one company, a gent who had been happily working for us out of Australia for almost a decade was summarily moved in a flash when the company received a polite note stating that since the gent was obviously not a temporary worker, when he crossed his tenth-year anniversary, the company would get the full bill for ten years of their version of Social Security and Medicare.

By the way, keep your passports safe, both during use and after. I know from experience. I forgot (jet-lagged) I had one in my hip pocket on returning from overseas and washed it. That made it totally kaput, and I had to start over from scratch! And they keep the damaged passport, so you lose that record of travel. It is important if you are in a position that needs a security clearance. I found this out one day when, doing a routine renewal, I was asked where I had been … and when … for the past decade. By this time, I had lived overseas for five years and been globe-trotting before and after for another five. We rescheduled, and I brought in all my passports—a several-inch stack of them. The interviewer's jaw dropped. We carefully went through all the legible entry/exit stamps to build my travel schedule to over a dozen countries for ten years. He said, almost under his breath, "There is no way they will renew your clearance." He was wrong. The next renewal had even more passports, but this time it was some kid on his first postcollege job. He said, "This is so cool!" and we still did the page-by-page thing, but this time with lots of "There I was …" stories to keep him entertained. Anyway, keep the passports safe. Speaking of which, have a printed file copy of all your past living addresses. You will need that as well, and if you have moved as frequently as I have over thirty years, the long-ago addresses fade. (That may just be my advancing chronological disability, however.)

Anyway, my time with the Aussies did end, and I then had to make a decision what to do. As it turns out, all those 401(k) savings over the years had piled up, and with some recent inheritance and passing the magic age of fifty-nine-and-a-half, I had more options than taking the first thing to come along. That is when the wife said, "Go do something with that PhD we paid a bundle for." I incorporated my own special (S) corporation to consult in offsets and countertrade—still international but focused on helping US companies go international, at least on one specific point.

Of course, one might ask why, with all its nebulousness in detail and vagueness in schedule, I would want to attempt to establish a consulting business in international business, especially offsets and countertrade. One honest reason is obviously that I have enjoyed working on international programs over the years. Coupled with experience and an expensive doctorate, I thought perhaps I could be of use to companies and countries. Second, in spite of saber (or treaty) rattling by various countries, no country is autarkic in its resources or its products. There has always been and will always be international trade. That is not going away. It may go up, as it did after the Cold War, and it may drop like a rock, as it did in the 1930s. But it will never be zero. Those who have the ability and inclination to trade or facilitate trade internationally will always have a chance for productive employment.

Specific to offsets, the world writ large is increasing its appetite for those aspects of offsets termed variously industrial collaboration, localization, technology transfer, and global supply chain entry. All these go beyond the simple, almost barter-like trade of goods. They result in complex deals touching export regulations, the ability of countries to effectively absorb the work or technology, the attitude of companies for transferring technology and investing time and money into international endeavors, and the willingness of countries to allow exports of technologies and investment. Over my years, I have seen a constant increase in country demands for real work and investment. Even the US can be on that bandwagon with its Buy American Act and its insistence that major government procurements have significant American-based value added. In fact, countries are now renaming their policies akin to the terms in this paragraph's first sentence. Fortunately, "collaboration" can still ring true, as none of those terms work without collaboration. Thank heavens that the search engine optimization tool on websites allows me to enter all the above terms so search engines can identify my website.

I therefore believe strongly that as countries seek to sharpen their industrial participation or collaboration policies, I will find work on one side of the table or the other. With my academic underpinning and my industry experience, I can help a country craft a more productive, more efficient policy. With all my experiences, I can help companies respond more effectively to these new policy goals. At least I am giving it a serious try. I had enough experience in enough places around the world to be of value to that set of other small and medium-sized businesses desiring to enter the international market and therefore run up against these various forms of an offset policy. Though, perhaps not all my experiences were directly applicable.

Going out to the Floating Buoy

There I was … another demo in the summer heat of the Middle East. We were asked to do a demonstration on a floating buoy being considered for early-warning coastal defense. Twice. No, three times. Oops—four times. It was a thirty-minute boat trip out. Because it floats, a nonstabilized system wouldn't work. But we had to demo it anyway, as it was cheaper. Then we brought out the smaller stabilized system. Good but didn't see far enough. So, we hauled out the big-dog system. On our first demo of it, we didn't bother to put it on top of the forty-foot-high buoy; we just set up the tripod on the floating buoy's main deck. However, the potential end user wanted it on top, so we had to make yet another trip out and haul it up the swaying tower in the middle of the Arabian Sea in the middle of the summer. As the boss, I had sacrificed the boys for the first couple of demos. But guilt was finally kicking in, so I felt I needed to pitch in for the last one, as we would be hauling a million-dollar, hundred-pound unit up about forty feet (not to mention risking dropping it into forty feet of salt water during the boat-to-buoy transfer sequence). The buoy, like all things maritime for more than a couple of days, was covered in seagull guano; it was not only slippery, it stank to high heavens once the day went from "just hot" to "convection oven." We got the demo done and put the video on the DVD to hand over for customer analysis.

The fascinating part was the discussion with the accompanying senior local, a midgrade officer. This kid (half my age, so I can say that) had more cars than I did on either of my two continents. He spoke perfect English. He also pitched in to help get the stuff up and down. Note that the buoy was absolutely guano covered. He had an interesting cultural story. He was on training in the US (either language or intelligence schools—can't remember) and had a neighboring country mate in the course. Except this classmate was a general; the kid was probably a first lieutenant at the time. At one point during the course, his classmate asked him to help buy a used car. This guy was thinking, *You are a general, and you can afford only a used car?* Truth will out—it was in fact true.

It was also the same interesting discussion where I learned about local government attempts to marry locals. These consisted at a minimum of heavily subsidized housing prices as well as monetary bonuses.

Moral: Well, sometimes you do, in fact, get a *shitty* job internationally—in this case, quite literally. My two prior Marines and I did fine, but my civilian gent lost it ... quite literally, though he continued to support the mission.

On setting up my own consulting business, the process has been fascinating and educational. First, lots of people are happy to take your money. From the lawyers who incorporated the company for me to insurance and a wide variety of web-based entities who help establish the company, we have laid out a fair bit of change. Some were bought for several years' running—for instance, the website via GoDaddy and WordPress. We have also had good support from the small business administrations of the state of Maryland, and we are now involved in both the state and federal Small Business Administration (SBA) efforts. The mailing lists are not always relevant, but often they do provide good information and excellent networking opportunities. Even more than in large business, networking is critical to growing one's name and brand recognition in the marketplace. Also, many organizations have help for small businesses—from low-interest loans to flat-out grants, especially if you are attempting to export your product or services. As mentioned prior, for instance, Maryland has a number of permanent overseas offices around the world to assist Maryland small businesses going abroad as well as recruit potential foreign entities into investing in Maryland.

The first thing we had to do was charter the company. We looked seriously at only two alternatives: a limited liability corporation or partnership (LLC/LLP) and the S corp—a full corporation but with restricted stockholders and a reduced board of directors' requirement. There are advantages and disadvantages to both. I didn't plan on taking on a partner in the near future, but when starting out, it seemed foolish to close that door immediately. My spouse was therefore included in the incorporation in roles she is especially good at, such as treasurer and secretary. She was going to mainly be a back-office type, worried about the funds and doing artwork as needed for presentations. The LLC would have been expandable outside the immediate family, of course, but it presents unique challenges on changing the size, especially on downsizing or dissolving it. The S Corp, while a bit more expensive to set up and more detailed in the administrative requirements needed (e.g., minutes of the board's meetings), it would more easily allow adding a restricted-rights partner, allow me to actually hire someone if desired, and a benefit I hadn't considered: if I make good, then I invite my children to join the board and start distributing funds via their share on the board. Once the company was set (and the lawyers paid to do so), we had a company, complete with stock certificates suitable for framing. This entire effort, from first visit to incorporation, took a bit over six weeks, and part of that was over the end-of-year holidays, so I suspect we lost at least two weeks in that regard.

Next on the list was to get business insurance. We had quotes from several companies and talked with a few that seemed most stable. We didn't get any big underwriters—looks like, for us, USAA didn't do business insurance, at least then. At a business conference later, the topic did come up informally and was confirmed, though there were already internal discussions ongoing, as USAA exists to serve active, retired, and veterans of all services—and the latter two were entering into more and more business. But we finally had three insurance certificates issued: general (oops, someone slips on your driveway walking in for a meeting); professional (oops, I told you do to your program this way, and you ignored me and lost but are blaming me anyway); and, on the recommendation of our website designer, cyber protection. The last was mainly to keep my website from being hacked, as I don't sell via my website. But he said he'd seen a lot of what can go wrong; so at least the insurance would fund rehosting somewhere else. It was the most expensive of the three—costing practically as much as the other two combined.

Moving on to the website, we elected to go with a small professional website designer. He has done an excellent job of taking our desires and making them work online. We did play with WordPress and Adobe, but we hadn't built a website in over a decade and a half, and the new tools and requirements have increased a hundredfold. We provided the words and artwork; he did the rest, including providing us with a detailed how-to for each step of setting up and validating the website. He liked the GoDaddy/WordPress combo, and we have been happy with them. The only gotcha is that in setting up the company for more than one person, we had to buy a premium Microsoft online package. We were wondering why my wife wasn't getting my emails; turns out the basic package was only one email. A few hundred dollars later, we both can now see everything. Speaking of which, we did play with the cloud for storage and exchange of files and data. In the end, for my small company, we have decided just to buy our own small server and do it ourselves. It is easier for us (with just two), and we'll save the cost of Adobe within a year. Final note: the web designer suggested we just hire him for a reasonable amount each year to do minor updates as they occur. He said he had tried to bill folks for each small job and decided it wasn't worth either parties' time. For a set amount once a year, I send him any notes I want changed (we are talking minor misspellings, or I updated my CV page), and off he does it, generally within twenty-four hours. A very convenient arrangement.

This, by the way, appears to be important for improving your search and hit rates. Google, for instance, likes websites that are secure (https) and that get updated with some degree of frequency. We opted in for a Small Business workshop on search engine optimization (SEO), and it was all new to us and invaluable. SEO is how search engines find your site, using key words and phrases in the SEO area—not necessarily in the main text. We were lucky, said the teacher, that our site was new and therefore still small. If you have been in business for a bit, adding in the SEO information and words (to dozens of pages, for instance) will be laborious.

As part of setting up the website, we elected to try a hand at online advertising. My area is a very niche area. But we went for a Google Ads account, even though I am not in the consumer market. I must say that Google Ads is tailor-made for a real or online storefront selling "stuff." My consultancy sees fewer direct benefits. But via Google Ads (pick the level with data available) and via Google Analytics (for free by clipping and sending some code to your webmaster), you get a good idea where in the world people are looking at you. Ads tracks key words as well, so you can eliminate the key words that are obviously not your area and get in the key words and phrases that are you. They track page views, retention and bounce rates, and geography. Also, Ads is trying to track gender and age (from what I can tell, doing okay, but it is irrelevant for me). You can also limit Ads to just the area you want to sell to. In my case, it is the whole world minus countries on prohibited lists. But if I had started a coffee shop, I could have been able to limit my Ads to just, say, the fifteen-block area around my store. I start every day by checking Analytics to see from where I have been visited and whether directly (i.e., someone knows me already), social (web browser or LinkedIn), or paid (my ad appeared due to a search, and the viewer clicked on). At least I know I am not being forgotten. I have also initiated a blog. Not sure how long I can keep it up, but by expanding a bit about what I write about, I'll certainly clear over a year of every other week. And the upload is easy. I do it myself via WordPress, even including pictures or graphics. I did find that Google Ads' "help" was of no help; they did not understand my business, and their attempts to help were not productive. Not surprising, given my niche specialty. I suspect for a more consumer or general business orientation, they would be useful. I have had to shut them down twice—not that they were making any further money off the site, just overeager to help with a business they knew absolutely nothing about. Hence, you are often your company's best business-development expert. Do not forget that.

At the same time as most of the above, we began to check with the state of Maryland's small business office for pointers and other thoughts. They have been uniformly helpful. To start, they have lots of free advice programs. When we couldn't get into our county's office promptly (folks on vacation or travel), they quickly moved us to a neighboring county, and we had an appointment within a week. The gent had been his own small business owner. He had a good checklist and went right down it. He covered many of the things we had already considered but also dwelt at length on state and federal programs designed to help small businesses. These not only included access to financing and some marketing assistance, but they also included—my interest—support going internationally. Since every state is different, I won't cover the specifics, but you should! Go set up a visit. I haven't met anyone in any of the state offices or meetings yet who wasn't full of info and zeal for my company.

They also, because of my international interest, introduced me to a US Department of Commerce program called the District Export Council (DEC). These folks are all small businesses wanting to export or having exported. They are there with ideas and experiences. Also, the DOC and DEC are always having speakers and networking sessions to help small companies grow.

Speaking of which, also remember to register with the Small Business Administration. They have ins to many small pots of support for small businesses. I also registered with the US government under a small business set-aside program under the Government Services Agency (GSA), which allows your company to be selected by either a government entity or a private entity looking to spend small business dollars. While you are at it, don't rule out a registration, if applicable, as a minority, female, veteran, and so on -owned small business. I am not too interested in USG contracts, and the paperwork to apply became a burden; even though the Veterans Administration office of small business verification always promptly answered the phone, they also always came up with yet more documents I needed to get the final verification. So, suit it to your business model; mine doesn't seriously include future federal business. But if you don't register, you can't even be considered. The programs are free.

There are also other programs out there. Your state and federal offices will help you find loans, for instance. I have only dabbled in that area, as I have gone to my financial advisor, whose company worked up an equity line of credit. Doesn't cost me a thing unless I tap into it, and it has other interesting features like no need to make a monthly payment. The idea is that you pull the funds to win the business and pay it back once you strike the gold. There are also more obscure areas to assist and insure you against unexpected costs or losses. For exports, there are small business set-asides to ensure payment that are managed by the Export-Import (EXIM) Bank. In these, once you have a contract, for a trivial percentage, EXIM will guarantee you get 90 percent of your contact value should the foreign entity not pay. This includes not only failure to pay due to obstinance or bankruptcy but impacts caused, for instance, by force majeure–type stuff like a major government policy change (theirs or ours), including embargos, confiscations, and nationalizations.

There is, of course, the routine of finding and joining appropriate organizations. My specialty doesn't have too many, being such a niche knowledge base, so I joined the only one that would have me. Even before I was officially notified of acceptance, I was called and asked to join the training committee. Turns out that good deeds do not go unpunished, and somehow they had remembered me from a decade prior when I was with some other company. Their training team needed a third person, and they thought I was the man for the job. Except this is a volunteer position, and the first class I was to help with was at the conference in

Europe. Well, Paris isn't at all bad in the spring, except for the cost to get there and back. I should have screwed it up, but I didn't, and now I am running the training. It is a fantastic networking opportunity. Speaking of which, don't overlook your alumni groups. They can also be fantastic networking groups, as I have found out with the service academies. We may be a little unique, but I don't think we are totally unique.

A few other IT-ish / web-ish tips. QuickBooks is a great way for a small business to start. It tracks everything for you and takes only a couple of weeks to get the basics down. If you have an accountant not living in the Stone Age, you can give them access to your account, and they have all the receipts and entries you have filed for the year—all ready to download, reorganize, and submit to the IRS. Since it links to your (company) bank and card, it keeps you honest and up-to-date. Next: Scannable, by Evernote. I was scanning my cards—laboriously, one by one—but not entering contact info. I had looked with envy on our tradeshow folks who did all that at the stand while waiting. On an associate's recommendation (who was more into IT than I was), I bought into Scannable. Not bad for a year. A phone-picture, and it lets you know if it understands it. If so, it recognizes it as a contact, and you can add it to your smartphone immediately. If not, you can still email yourself both the card scan and a Scannable v-card guess, which my Outlook normally recognizes and adds even with some corrections. And you can still then save the actual scanned card on your local server. Finally, there are several online legal form providers as well as a host of CDs at an office supply store. I went online, and for a fair price, I had unlimited access to their forms. The forms are fillable and editable. As a very small consulting business, they have mainly been of use evaluating them as a boilerplate against potential contracts, nondisclosure agreements, and other agreements to see if all the bases are covered.

I will wind down with how I came to write this book. I have always wanted to write a book of some sort. My first attempt was back in high school, a swords and sorcery fantasy attempt. It went nowhere except in copied form to a few close friends. At the Naval Academy, I took a class in creative writing (got an A). One of my short stories was considered good enough by my professor to make a run at publication. I paid a secretary to type it up properly and sent it off to a series of pulp fiction magazines to test interest. Unfortunately, no nibbles. I gave up on writing a book, though not on the dream of writing a book. But over the years, I was able to have several master's papers published in appropriate professional journals and a few technical articles published in the company technical field journal. On finishing my doctorate, I began to toy with the idea of transforming the thesis into a book. That didn't seem as interesting (or as easy) as I thought it might be, especially given its narrow focus. However, on starting my company and associated website, I started my blog. After several months, my wife encouraged me to consider wrapping my blog and my experiences into a book that would be both fun and educational to read—hence this tome.

I did not envision myself becoming a serial author, so I sought out several websites to help with the publishing and let them do the hard stuff (formatting, editing, distribution). As part of that effort, they recommended I join something call the Author Learning Center, which, for a very trivial fee, gives you access to lots of "how to write a book of various genres" info. On that website, they actually debate which way to go—self or publishing house. It is interesting, but as of this printing, I am happy with my determination to not go it alone. Writing has been tough enough. The publisher I selected (Archway) has been supportive and communicative. I obviously cannot tell at this point how the marketing will go, but here is hoping they are as effective there as they have been so far! And, in case you missed it, my wife did the art. A labor of both love and frustration. She enjoyed it tremendously, and she feels like she is contributing as much or more to the success of the company as she ever did to my corporate career. (Which is a shame, as she contributed a lot to that, just in other ways.)

So, as the chapter title says, I am now off on a new course, a good portion of it in uncharted waters. The adventure still beckons, and I hope I find that pot of gold at the end of the rainbow … and not the falls at the edge of the earth.

I have had some younger folks ask me, "How do I get into international business? It sounds so exciting!" I hope my stories have helped put that line of work into somewhat of a new perspective. Yes, it is exciting—at times. At other times, it is exhausting, boring, lonely, frustrating, confusing, and even a bit scary.

Exhausting, because you travel a tremendous amount of the time (except, perhaps, if you are an expatriate with a single country focus). Jet travel has gotten better in some respects with quieter and more humid cabins. But I still walk off a plane drinking a liter of water. Even in business class, you will find it difficult to sleep—and business class is a disappearing policy as companies go to shave pennies off the bottom line of costs. This in spite of their desire to have you walk off a plane and into a meeting—to save the extra night's hotel stay. On your return, the expectation is usually to either stop by the office on the way home or "be there all the earlier the next day," to quote Scrooge. I have literally seen folks nose-dive into their dinner soup they were so tired.

Boring, because as connected as the world is, you spend a lot of time waiting: waiting at airports, waiting for meetings that are delayed, waiting while the customer takes a break, and even waiting for that call to meet that may or may not come. General connectivity increases in the past decade have helped reduce this aspect some. Most airlines now have connectivity even in flight, not to mention a hundred movies and TV programs and games. And unless your cell phone has to remain outside the office, you can still be productive in your emails or take calls or read an e-book (like this one, perhaps).

Lonely, because you will not be constantly entertained while on the road. Have good books or e-books, your favorite movies, or start a(no-ther) graduate degree like I did to fill those quiet nights in a hotel room. Sure, your representative, your local colleague, and maybe even your customer will get you out a bit—but not every night of a seven-day stay. They have families too.

Frustrating, because international deals rarely close as quickly as domestic transactions. First, there are the administrative burdens of the contract negotiations—often in another language or dual language. Then there is the fact, especially in a government or government-related contract, that they have the same or even greater budgetary restrictions and concerns than ours. Decisions often have to flow to the highest levels for large programs, and those individuals have many demands on their time and many departments clamoring for their contracts to be finally approved internally.

Confusing, because both local procurement decisions and US export decisions are not entirely logical. For the local government, many needs must be met from a single pot of funds. Therefore, what often looks like a "sure thing, gotta have this system" fails on larger issues. For the US input, decisions are made month-on-month. Hit a bad stretch of human rights, and you may be out of luck.

Scary, in that a lot of the world is on a precarious edge of safe versus anarchy. The Huns, Goths, Mongols, and others finally figured out—over centuries—that poor but unspoiled serfs paid more than raiding each village. But this took a long time. Collecting taxes is far less glorious than riding into battle—something proven as recently as the Daesh attempt to take over a chunk of the Syria/Iraq border. Even with social media helping recruit, both the slave wives and fighters finally realized that they were getting nothing but death and it was time to quite literally go home.

Exciting, yes—for me, it has been quite exciting! I may have lived a unique life, but I have met numerous others also living that unique life. The cultural exposure is without fail a huge attraction. Living the life—whether local (e.g., Peace Corps) or business (e.g., corporate ex-patriate)—you still get a huge immersion into the culture surrounding your assignment. From national mosques to Christmas markets to Hindu temples, you gather a greater appreciation of the diversity available to beliefs and practices in humankind. I had the chance—finally—to see more than the city on a trip to Bangalore. Several colleagues joined me on a trip to Mysore, capital of one of the last non-British kingdoms in India. Part of the trip was a stop at a famous Hindu temple—which, thanks to my years in Malaysia and associated ethnic Indian friends, I was able to help navigate in an intelligent manner. The hard part is trying to remember to wish all your various friends the proper holiday greeting at the appropriate time! Social media helps, and once you are on a list of, for instance, former classmates, you can easily send a note—but you have to remember to do so. Start adding in various independence days (yes, guess what—not every country was formed on the Fourth of July—go figure), and you almost have a full-time job just wishing your friends a happy holiday.

As for getting into this line of work, there are no easy answers. As indicated by my book's title, I kind of fell into the role over numerous years. I have one colleague whose missionary parents set him up for a very unique position linguistically as well as experientially for a future in international business. But that is the rare exception. For your standard American, you have to look for the opportunities as they come along. You also have to be willing to except some risk and some nebulousness in the details of the assignment. One of the positions I filled was for a previously considered candidate who had an aging mother living with him with some medical issues that could not be guaranteed in the overseas environment. Out he went from consideration, and in I came as the guy for the job. As you should have gathered from my various stories, flexibility is a key ingredient to international business—whether doing it or being considered for it.

I will close with a few final words on the subject. If you are unable to sympathize or empathize with other cultures or points of view, stay away from international business. You do not have to agree with their points of view or cultural positions. But you absolutely must be able to understand those views and adjust your responses as appropriate to conclude the business at hand. Otherwise, you are facing a major obstacle in concluding a deal. The competition will likely have more empathetic marketing people who can create that bond—however tenuous—to conclude the deal. Listen. Listening is critical. The old saw about God giving us two ears and one mouth to suggest priority is especially true in international transactions. Choose your words carefully *after* you have *listened* to the customer. Do not fear the pregnant silent pause; it is critical in establishing your credibility as an international business partner.

Finally, enjoy the trip. You never know where the voyage will take you. I would never have guessed over a decade in Asia in one area or another. As several of my chronologically challenged friends have said, "When I am no longer having fun, I quit." That should be your motto as well.

Acronym List

24/7/365   twenty-four hours a day, seven days a week, 365 days a year (i.e., all the time)
9/11   reference to the terrorist attacks in the US on September 11, 2001
AC   air-conditioning
ASAP   as soon as possible
ATM   automatic teller machine
BAFO   best and final offer
BCE   before Common Era (old BC—before year 1)
CBP   Customs and Border Patrol
CIA   Central Intelligence Agency
CD   compact disc
DEC   District Export Council (regional USG/SBA entity to help small businesses go international)
DKF   Deutches Kompensations Forum (Germany-based offset organization)
DMZ   demilitarized zone
DOC   Department of Commerce
EAR   Export Administration Regulations
EXIM   Export Import Bank
FCPA   Foreign Corrupt Practices Act
GPA   grade point average
GSA   General Services Administration (USG purchasing entity)
ID   identification
IRS   Internal Revenue Service
IT   information technology
ITAR   International Traffic in Arms Regulations
JSF/F-35   Joint Strike Fighter, official nomenclature F-35
LLC/LLP   limited liability corporation/partnership
MiG   generic reference to Soviet/Russian fighters, specifically from the Mikoyen-Gurevich design bureau
MOD   ministry of defense
NAFOD   no apparent fear of death

NOAA	National Oceanic and Atmospheric Administration
OFAC	Office of Foreign Assets Control
OMG	oh my God
PRC	People's Republic of China
RIO	radar intercept officer (back seat in an F-4 Phantom)
SBA	Small Business Administration
S corp	a corporation organized under Subchapter S of IRS Code Chapter 1
SEC	Securities and Exchange Commission
SEO	search engine optimization
STEP	Smart Traveler Enrollment Program
SUNY	State University of New York
TSA	Transportation Security Administration
UAE	United Arab Emirates
UK	United Kingdom
US	United States of America
USAA	United Services Automobile Association
USAF	United States Air Force
USN	United States Navy
USG	United States government
USMC	United States Marine Corps
VIP	very important person
VP	vice president

Mentioned Military Equipment:

Cargo Aircraft: (US) C-130 Hercules

Tactical Aircraft:

US: A-4E & TA-4J Skyhawk, A-6 Intruder, A-7 Corsair II, E-2 Hawkeye, F-4 Phantom II, F-14 Tomcat, F-16 Falcon, F/A-18 Hornet
Non-US: Saab 35 DRAKEN, Saab JAS 39 GRIPEN, MiG-21 Fishbed, MiG-23 Flogger, MiG-29 Fulcrum, SU-30 Flanker
Aircraft Carrier: USS *Midway*, CV-41

Index

About the Author

Dr. Alan Colegrove has been in the international arena for more than forty years. After serving seven years as a Navy fighter pilot, he entered the defense-aerospace industry, spending most of thirty years in international business. He has lived three times overseas, has advanced academic degrees from three continents, and has traveled to more than four dozen countries, doing business in about half of them. His experiences include East Asia, the Middle East, and Europe. His doctorate was in an obscure branch of defense economics known as offsets and countertrade. Dr. Colegrove currently resides in Maryland on the Chesapeake Bay with his wife of more than thirty-five years. He has two grown children (who, when younger, lived overseas with him on one of his assignments) and one grandchild.

Printed in the United States
By Bookmasters